Praise for *Own Your Anxiety*

"As an ER doctor in a trauma center who has seen thousands of patients' stressful situations, I can attest that *Own Your Anxiety* places powerful tools to change your relationship with anxiety and stress at your fingertips. Julian has taken on a serious issue with intelligence, artfulness, care, and relatability, and created a work that serves as a vibrant tool chest for those wanting to enrich their inner environments in hard times."

DR. MICHAEL MCCULLOUGH, emergency room doctor, University of California, San Francisco; investor; and founder of BrainMind

"Along with exercise, meditation, and eating right (all of which you'll find out more about in these pages), reading the right books is one of my top ways to manage anxious feelings that can otherwise stifle a life. *Own Your Anxiety* is an ultra-positive read giving us hope that each day is a new day that a person who is suffering can cope and lead a healthier life. Julian is a guide that you just want to spend time with. He's been there, knows how to work through anxiety, and can help you work through it, too. Read this book!"

JESSICA MULRONEY, marketing expert, entrepreneur, and fashion contributor for *Good Morning America* and *CityLine*

"Wow—what a powerful book. At a time when so many are experiencing existential angst and may at times feel paralyzed by anxiety or other mental health challenges, comes a thoughtful, accessible, and empathetic book that provides a practical road map for building a better life. I would recommend this book to anyone who is working on becoming their better self."

JULIA CHRISTENSEN HUGHES, founding dean, Gordon S. Lang School of Business and Economics at the University of Guelph

"As an athlete, I face the 'fight-or-flight' anxiety mode daily, understanding anxiety and how to control it has become my greatest asset. The skills I have learned from reading this book carry me forward."

KAILLIE HUMPHRIES, two-time Olympic gold medal champion and first female bobsledder to defend her Olympic title

"In an era of social media madness comes a voice of reason, with practical suggestions regarding how to de-stress, refocus, and take control of our lives. Julian provides 99 simple tips to reclaim your body, mind, and soul, which can help the walking wounded to live, not just exist. This is not a self-help book per se, but rather a thoughtful guide to enable self-reflection and self-awareness, one that is timely and practical."

DR. BARRY KOSOFSKY, chief neurologist and Goldsmith Professor of Neuroscience, Weill Cornell Medical Center; chief pediatric neurologist, New York-Presbyterian/Komansky Children's Hospital

"You are so worthy of everything you desire. You are so worthy of living your dreams. And you are so worthy of learning how to use your anxiety as your natural fuel—Julian Brass' *Own Your Anxiety* will show you how!"

MELISSA AMBROSINI, bestselling author, speaker, podcaster, and spiritual teacher

"Each section of *Own Your Anxiety* is written more brilliant than the next, each word more pointed than the last—all so obvious that it makes you wonder how so many little things can have such a huge impact on our lives and the lives around us. This book reminds me that we as people can't control everything; there will be good, there will be bad, there will be mistakes, but we are never alone."

DEBRA MARGLES, president, Michael Kors Canada

"Julian lays out digestible techniques to utilize the superpower that is anxiety. He takes a holistic approach in helping the reader befriend the urgency for the greatness anxiety can inspire while offering help to tame the 'my wheels are spinning so fast, I may lose control' sensation."

CONNOR CARRICK, NHL defenseman

"Julian has been a valued speaker at Wanderlust for several years. His clear message and ability to connect has had a profound impact on our attendees, and we're excited (but not anxious, since he's helped with that) to hear more from him."

SEAN HOESS, CEO and cofounder, Wanderlust Festival

"*Own Your Anxiety* is a sacred resource for anyone working through anxiety in our modern world. Julian offers us a safe space full of enriching inspiration and practical tools to enhance our experience of every single day."

ELENA BROWER, bestselling author of *Practice You*

"Anxiety is everywhere. Whether you personally deal with anxiety or care for someone who is afflicted by this condition, this is a must-read."

BERTRAND CESVET, CEO, Sid Lee

"From career to personal, anxiety can be a positive driving force in your life or a negative distraction. *Own Your Anxiety* will take you on an entertaining journey of personal and spiritual growth and teach you practical tools that will elevate your life."

ERAN ELFASSY, founder and co-creative director, Mackage

"Julian has successfully communicated, through an honest journey of his own life experiences, that anxiety is a natural and useful state. One that we need to understand and manage like any other emotion. Our chaotic and overstimulated lives have prevented us from taking time to listen to and trust ourselves. This book reminds us how."

ELAINE KUNDA, founder and managing partner, Disruption Ventures

"Giving is living. This has been the guiding philosophy for us at Bombas. And this is exactly what Julian has done in *Own Your Anxiety*. He's offered the world a relatable and practical method to enhance the lives of people living with anxiety regardless of social class or income status. This book is for everyone—that's why I love it!"

DAVID HEATH, cofounder and CEO, Bombas

"As a family medicine physician, a large part of my practice involves treating anxiety and depression. It is rare to find a resource as clear, non-judgmental, relevant, applicable, and most importantly, as genuine as *Own Your Anxiety* by Julian Brass. I am excited to offer my patients this great resource as a supplemental tool in their search to manage their anxiety."

DR. RAVEENA SEETAL, BSC, MD, AAFP, CFPC

"The conversation around healthy ways to own anxiety is needed today more than ever, and I am happy to see that Julian has dedicated himself to helping people change their relationship with anxiety. Anything Julian puts himself into makes an impact. Want to be impacted? Read this book!"

W. BRETT WILSON, chairman, Prairie Merchant; former Dragon, *Dragons' Den*

"This book is a great resource for anyone who wishes to learn some of the many techniques and secrets to success in dealing with everyday anxiety and stress."

ISRAEL SCHACHTER, cofounder and CEO, CharityBids

"*Own Your Anxiety* is the ultimate intro guide to daily life in our modern stressful world. Julian has generously curated for us a fun and comprehensive list of simple tips for our body, mind, and soul. I highly recommend this book to anyone who is ready to start taking care of their emotional well-being!"

MIRI POLACHEK, CEO, Joy Ventures

"In order to truly Think and Grow Rich in all aspects of your life, you must work on your mental health. Julian's methods of owning anxiety are amazing! They are practical, easy to do, and will make a significant impact on you mental and physical well-being. I highly recommend this to all my students as these methods are for almost all ages! If you have been struggling with anxiety or if you want to take your mental health to the next level, this book is for you!"

SUNNY VERMA, CEO, TutorBright and Think and Grow Rich Institute

"Learning how to master your anxious feelings is a key part of living your BEST LIFE EVER! This book will give you the tools to shift your relationship with anxiety and stress in real time and it will help you lessen their occurrences altogether. Having this book in your collection will allow you to reference the lessons when needed and share them with the people you care about."

JAY M. KLEIN, founder, The PUR Company

"Of all the things that resonate with me in this book, perhaps most is the thought that 'somewhere' we really do know what's best for us, and when we have those anxious moments that we all do, it's our own higher self who is speaking to us. If we find ourselves becoming more anxious it's because we're not listening! From the whisper to the scream, we have the choice to hear the inner voice and change the dialogue. What Julian has done in this book is encourage us on multiple levels to find a harmonious balance with our mind, body, and soul!"

RON REID, owner and director of Downward Dog Yoga Centre, teaching internationally since 1995

"Julian's intimate understanding of entrepreneurship, nutrition, fitness, yoga, spirituality, and wellness is something that anyone can relate to regardless of where they're at in their life, and his strategies in *Own Your Anxiety* will give you tools that work for YOU!"

GREG O'GALLAGHER, president, Kinobody; @gregogallagher

"Anxiety is a problem that affects everyone. Julian has found practical and effective ways for people to develop mechanisms on how to view this topic and also how to manage it. *Own Your Anxiety* is a great guide into how to change our mindsets, and to see things in a different light."

CHITRA ANAND, author, keynote speaker, professor, and advisor to high-growth companies

99 SIMPLE WAYS
TO CHANNEL
YOUR SECRET EDGE

JULIAN BRASS

FOREWORD BY **JOE MIMRAN**
Founder of Club Monaco and Joe Fresh

OWN
YOUR
ANXIETY

PAGE TWO
BOOKS

ISBN 978-1-989025-62-8 (paperback)
ISBN 978-1-989025-63-5 (ebook)

Page Two
www.pagetwo.com

Cover and interior design by Peter Cocking
Back cover photograph by Javier Mereb
Interior photographs by Darius Bashar
Printed and bound in Canada by Friesens
Distributed in Canada by Raincoast Books
Distributed in the US and internationally by
Publishers Group West, a division of Ingram

19 20 21 22 23   5 4 3 2 1

OwnYourAnxiety.com
#OwnYourAnxiety
JulianBrass.com
@JulianBrass

This book is not intended as a substitute for the medical advice of
physicians. The reader should regularly consult a physician
in matters relating to his/her health and particularly with respect to
any symptoms that may require diagnosis or medical attention.

This book is dedicated to YOU.

You are limitless, strong, and full of love.

We're ALL in this together.

Contents

• • • • •

Foreword

JULIAN BRASS is on a mission to make a true impact on the lives of people who want to live better, regardless of their anxiety, stress, or mental health challenges. His book, *Own Your Anxiety*, offers everyone simple ways to quickly manage those challenges, irrespective of their social class, geographical location, or physical abilities.

This book will guide you to own your anxiety—and even to own your entire life! It presents a journey toward self-improvement and self-finding. Contained within these pages is Julian's story of being completely lost, breaking, and then picking up the pieces to put himself back together as a better version of his former self. He reminds you to honor yourself, by sharing about times when he didn't honor himself. But this book is not only his journey; it is yours, too. I love this book because it is so relatable and so honest! Julian doesn't let us forget that even when times feel really scary, hard, and lonely—times that, as a serial entrepreneur, I have intimate knowledge of—we can always create a healthy fire within ourselves to serve as our guiding light on the path to inner peace, success, and happiness.

Now more than ever, we need to know how to own our anxiety. In today's highly charged environment, where we are always connected, the ability to find moments to de-stress and deal with anxious situations and feelings has never been more important. The phenomena of constantly interacting with technology, devices, and the world through social media and the like is not restricted to entrepreneurs and professionals alone. It has reached into every strata of society, with youth hit particularly hard. But sometimes all we need is to become mindful and check in with ourselves, so that we can take that deep breath and learn to unwind.

Julian's message is truly universal and needed for so many people today. And he articulates this message in a way that anyone can understand. This is a rare skill set that, frankly, is just hard to find.

How many successful professionals have made time to hit their "pause button" to seek out sage learnings from Western science and Eastern traditions?

How many award-winning founders of super-popular online lifestyle magazines who are constantly in the spotlight leave it all behind? How many travel far from home to train with health and wellness practitioners, yoga gurus, and spiritual leaders around the world?

How many people who seemingly "have it all" are willing to leave it all and dedicate their lives to a path of service, helping others take charge of *their* lives and *their* anxiety?

This is something that I really respect about Julian.

While other books talk about how to "get rid of" or how to "heal yourself" from anxiety, this book teaches you about how to *own it. Own Your Anxiety* will inspire you to design an intentional lifestyle and a general way of being that shifts your challenges into conveniences, obstacles into opportunities, and problems into potential. Julian has created a successful life, both in business and personally, by learning how to change his relationship with anxiety, to make it his secret edge—and so can you!

This work by Julian Brass will put you on the path to do just that.

Now it is your turn.

Here's to truly being the owner of every part of your life. You can be. You deserve to be.

With great respect,

JOE MIMRAN
Founder of Club Monaco and Joe Fresh

Your Secret Edge

I T'S AN EPIDEMIC. It's sweeping through our communities, homes, schools, and workplaces. Many sufferers are silent while others don't even know what's wrong with them or how to fix it.

I'm talking about . . . anxiety.

Often it feels like it's bigger than we are and that it's just too much to handle, so we try to "cope" with it. We try to "make do" with it. This is no way to live. I know because I tried living like this for too long. I was a mess.

This book is about owning your anxiety rather than being owned by it. It's about seeing that anxiety is a gift, an invitation to a better way of living.

Sometimes we try to beat our stresses and worries altogether. Another pill. Another prescription refill. Another glass. Another boozy night out. Another line. Another bite. Another fling. We've become a pill generation, medicated for anxiety *before* we intentionally attempt to see if there's something it's trying to tell us or if there's a natural way to manage it.

But what if anxiety is not a burden at all but is a unique gift? What if that tension we feel is in fact a powerful force of energy that we, *the anxious*, possess and that other so-called *normal* people don't?

What if our anxiety, when channeled in the right way, can give us an edge? What if that edge is our secret to helping us accomplish our greatest dreams, those that most people can't even conjure? What if that rush of nervous energy we sometimes feel, that adrenaline, is a blessing? What if it's all supposed to be this way? What if there's a way to not just survive but to *thrive* with anxiety?

I believe that there is. And I know it's possible for anyone, because it worked for me.

Do you know the intrusive feeling of waking up in the morning and having a small or not-so-small anxiety attack over breakfast for no reason at all? I do. Do you recognize that familiar sensation of butterflies in your stomach (and beyond) before you're about to give a speech or a presentation? I do. And what about that annoying and embarrassing eye twitch or overheating in a restaurant for no good reason? Familiar? Yes. Me, too.

Don't worry. You are not alone. Many people with anxiety have these experiences. But by becoming mindful and self-aware, suddenly you might see an opportunity to take control and get to the source of what you're feeling. This book is meant to help you find the source of the fire instead of just turning off the smoke alarm. Think of anxiety as your life sensor. What is it trying to tell you when it goes off?

Throughout your journey with this book, take time for self-reflection. I encourage you to ask yourself, "What is my anxiety trying to tell me?" Stay present. Let being present and awake become a way of empowered, conscious living that creates a confident awareness around the choices you make.

Anxiety became my life sensor when I started listening with intention to it. When I'm in the midst of an anxiety attack, I see the moment for what it is. I get empowered by the messages my body and mind are sending me. I listen. And then I decide what I'm going to do with the information. Because I'm mindful, I have the opportunity to decide what to do about my anxiety—and this is where it gets awesome.

Let's say you're about to go on stage in front of a group of people (could be at a wedding or for something related to work) and you're feeling seriously anxious. Or imagine you're about to take an exam (maybe for a course or certification that's really important to you) and you're overcome by anxiety. It spikes your nerves and travels throughout your body. It could manifest when you're about to have a defining and difficult conversation with someone—maybe it's a partner, employer, or client—and it's giving you clammy hands, heart hiccups, dry mouth. Maybe you're having trouble sleeping, which makes *everything* harder.

With this book, you're going to understand natural ways to take those nerves and turn them into energy that gives you clarity, creativity, and focus. You'll learn doable strategies that anyone—yes, that includes *you*—can start doing right now to transform that anxiety into a positive force. How much better would that be?

By reading this book, you'll learn natural lifestyle tips to *own what you're feeling* so that you access vibrant, amazing energy and even spread it to others around you.

I've got you. I've got your back.

Your Edge

Own Your Anxiety is the "manifestation" of the past eleven years of my life. I never knew myself to be anxious, but when I hit twenty-four years old and launched my former company, Notable, I came face to face with some of the scariest, loneliest anxious thoughts and states that I have ever known. Fear of the unknown will do that. I was unsure what my future held. I was living on canned tuna, Kraft Singles, and crackers. Making rent on time was top of mind. Once, while going to withdraw $40 from the ATM, my transaction slip said minus $36. I'll never forget the feeling of overwhelming anxiety entering every crevice of my body. Never.

My apartment looked like a scene from the movie *A Beautiful Mind* with Russell Crowe. The walls were covered with oversized white paper with goals and ideas for my new business, wireframes of what the website would look like, mantras and affirmations of what I hoped to create one day. I was a young man who desperately longed to "make it," but I lacked the holistic strategies to do that in a healthy, sustainable way.

Malnourished because I lacked money for quality food, I made things worse several nights a week. I would work until 10 p.m. and then get an invite from my "party friends" who owned the hottest nightclubs to join them for a night on the town. As a way of blowing off some steam and getting out of my depressing living situation, I'd soon be tableside in the booth taking shots, chugging vodka Red Bulls, and experimenting with drugs. The party nights would turn into party mornings spent in someone's mansion, penthouse, or condo. Sound glamorous? It wasn't. It was dark. Lonely. Fake.

Often after a party night and only three or four hours of sleep, my alarm would go off and I'd have to haul myself out of bed to go to work, which was literally at the desk beside my bed or a coffee shop outside. Run-down from sleep deprivation, hungover, and coming down from the "party favors," I'd rush for double or triple espressos, somehow find the strength to squeeze in an intense, adrenaline-pumping workout (knowing how desperately I needed the energy), and then take a freezing cold shower because I read somewhere that this would wake me up. Did I feel any better after all that? No.

I was in a shitty relationship with life. I was addicted to highs and lows. Times were tough, but my ridiculous habits were making them *even harder*. Anxiety, stress, and bouts of depression eventually became the new normal for me. I was constantly worried, even though I played it cool. You couldn't see it from the outside, but I had butterflies in my stomach most of the time, stomach aches, sweats coming out of nowhere, an annoying eye twitch, and I was literally hooked on caffeine and getting sick all the time.

I needed to regain control of my life. I needed to realize that the anxiety I was running from—because I thought it was hurting me—was my friend. I just had to learn how to listen to it. It took many years of slowly but surely embarking on a path of holistic, mindful living that brought me close to health professionals and spiritual gurus, and faith in a higher purpose. I began to tune in to my inner voice and values, and ultimately I learned that anxiety was an internal alarm trying to alert me that I was on the wrong path. By listening to when I got anxious and why, I learned about my triggers. I responded by either changing my lifestyle to avoid anxiety-causing situations or evolving my inner dialogue to turn the volume down on anxiety-causing thoughts. Learning how to live like this and to just listen to my anxiety is how I learned to:

Own Anxiety.

And now, I'm here to help you #OwnYourAnxiety.

That's what this book and this method of living are all about. I'm here to show you how to own your anxiety. Not just to live with it but literally *to like living with anxiety*. And eventually, you'll even learn how to channel it into a positive stream of renewable energy that will help you achieve your goals. Then one day, if you're like me, you might even appreciate it for what it is, this thing you used to see as holding you back—it's your gift. Anxiety is your secret edge.

Today, I put this idea into practice every day of my life. So much of this book was written during an exceptionally anxiety-filled period for me: helping my single, amazing mother fight the ferociously unfair cancer battle. As the only one of her children living in the same city, a lot of the responsibility to help was on me. And I had to rise to the occasion. I had to own my anxiety. On those dark, cold Canadian winter mornings on my way to pick her up for chemo appointments, the only choice was to own it. I had to channel my anxiety into an empathetic strength and resilience. I needed to put on my game face as I held her hand and we awaited the anxiety-ridden test results. I had to transform that energy into a secure loving-kindness as I shaved her head for the first time, once the effects of chemo started to overtake her body. And after her operation, when I had to pull the sticky, blood-soaked bandages off her breast as tears welled up in my eyes, nausea overtook my stomach, and butterflies flew rapidly in my chest, all the self-talking dialogue—you can imagine what would go through a thirty-five-year-old man's mind in this situation—simply had to be owned. In that moment, I had to own my anxiety in order to be calm, gentle, and compassionate. My intention with this book is that you will learn how to own your anxiety, no matter what life throws at you, too.

Maybe you can't imagine that right now. I recently spoke with someone who sought help in handling anxiety. This individual was so upset and overwhelmed by tears, which he kept apologizing for.

"Don't apologize for crying," I said. "Those tears are sacred. They're your insides speaking to you in their unique way. They're tears of awakening. You can't be scared when you're sacred," I shared.

Have you ever felt what my friend felt—imprisoned by your own anxiety and sadness? Maybe you're feeling as though you can't escape or that you're one million pounds or overwhelmed by and scared of the unknown. But I'm here to tell you that I've been there, and I'm here for you, right now, and I'm not leaving you. I know these horrid feelings, too. But I won't give up on you.

It may be pretty rough where you're at, but don't give up on yourself either. Stay with me here. Learn the strategies that I learned and that improved every aspect of my life.

I'm not going to say that by following this method you'll never feel overpowering anxiety again. That might be as close to impossible as it gets. But fully managing anxiety and thriving with it instead of going up against it *is* possible. It can happen in a moment, simply by having the right tools at your disposal. My goal with this book isn't to cure you of feelings of extreme, misguided energy, or what we commonly refer to as anxiety. My goal is to help you learn how to manage and channel that energy.

This book gives you the tools—doable lifestyle strategies that are at your fingertips. I'm talking about small changes to your daily habits so that you look at how you sleep, move, think, drink, eat, and love differently. You'll learn how to live in a way that doesn't bring on anxiety. You'll learn to handle whatever anxiety flare-ups come your way.

I've broken this book down into bite-sized lessons in three parts: Own Your Body, Own Your Mind, and Own Your Soul.

By the end of my method, you will wake up and go to sleep differently. You will walk and move differently. You will think and breathe differently. You will eat and drink differently. You will be you, but enhanced, evolved, and, yes, different—in a very good way. People will come to you for inspiration and advice, noticing how you've changed, and for the better. Why? Because anxiety has become your compass. Anxiety is your secret edge.

THIS BOOK IS for people who, at a non-clinical level, are suffering from anxious and stressful feelings. For many, the ways to own your anxiety that I share in this book will be just what you need to begin the joyous process of shifting your relationship with anxiety forever. But these methods aren't intended to be a substitute for medical advice. If you feel that you have a serious condition, make the first line of communication with your family doctor. If you're in an emergency situation, please visit a hospital immediately. There is no reason to ever be ashamed or embarrassed.

PART 1

OWN YOUR BODY

· · · · · · · ·

YOUR BODY is a blessing. It's sacred. Your body is brilliant. It's your personal gateway to your mind, and it knows and endures so much. It is the wisest machine that you may ever have, constantly sending you real-time, astute feedback. Your body is the vehicle that carries you through life. However, it is not the type of vehicle that you can just "trade in" to take a lease out on another. Your body is yours to keep, through good times and bad. Sometimes, you may forget to treat it like the temple that it is—and that's when your body will send you signals. These signals can be unpleasant and launch anxiety sky-high.

The good news is that you already possess sacred tools that can immediately begin to make your body feel better than ever. When you use these tools, you'll empower yourself. Imagine feeling better in your body than you ever have before. You're about to.

Part 1 of our journey together will teach you medically validated, extensively researched, totally doable, natural ways to treat your body so that you can own your anxiety for life.

Breathe

THEY SAY that the most common fear besides death is public speaking.

Picture this: in a few hours, you have a big presentation in front of ten or one thousand people. This presentation is a big deal. A lot depends on it. It gets your nerves going in a huge way; it makes you feel exceptionally anxious. How are you breathing? Are you breathing slow and deep, as if you're catching some rays on the beach, or is it more like you're running from a hungry tiger in the Sahara? Don't worry. We've all been there. It's no fun to feel this kind of high-level anxiety, especially when there are no tigers (at least no literal ones) about to take you down. Your body—and your breathing—is in what is commonly known as *emergency response*, or fight-or-flight.

So what are you supposed to do? How are you supposed to quell those pre-presentation nerves? Is that even possible? Yes. Yes, it is.

**Breath is the opponent of stress
and the enemy of anxiety.**

Breath enables us to go from emergency response to *relaxation response*. In high-anxiety situations, we tend to have high-intensity, fast-paced breathing. We are in fight-or-flight mode. We're acting like we're fleeing death, even if we're just waiting to do our big presentation or we're jetting to a date and we're going to be late or we're doing absolutely nothing. Making you anxious just thinking about it? Me, too! It makes me feel really *frigging* anxious.

But here's the antidote. The ancient yogis believed that the number of breaths we take determines our life span, more equals less—meaning that people who breathe many shallow, quick breaths for years on end will have a shorter life span than those who take long, deep, slow breaths. Studies have been done comparing breath rates and life spans, and compelling information definitely supports the "long breath, long life" idea.

For the moment, consider that breath is a skill. Not only that, it's a skill that can help you transform anxiety into a feeling of chill calm. Notice that I'm not asking you to do something really difficult here—no triathlons or intense math. Just . . . breathe.

Here's how:

Step 1: Place one hand on your belly as you begin inhaling through your nose. Direct the breath to the belly (below your chest). Feel your belly expand.

Step 2: Fill your belly to full capacity, meaning smoothly explore close to the edge of what you can comfortably hold.

Step 3: Once you've taken a full and complete breath in, exhale slowly and smoothly through your nose, allowing your belly to naturally contract without pushing or straining.

Remember the
nose-to-belly
breath and
you will always
be stronger than
your anxiety.

. . . .

Step 4: Repeat the in-breath and out-breath ten times or as many times as you need to regulate your breathing, calm your nerves, and appreciate the beautiful air that's part of our incredible universe.

Four simple steps—that's it! Or, made even simpler, breathe in fully, exhale fully, *live* fully. I call this *nose-to-belly* (NTB) breathing. Remember that! It's my goal that NTB breathing becomes second nature for you.

Research has proven that when we breathe deeply and consciously like this, and when we use our nostrils for both inhaling and exhaling, we activate our parasympathetic nervous system, which is associated with rest and relaxation. On the other hand, when breathing quickly through the mouth, we activate the sympathetic nervous system, the survival system that helps us escape from dangerous fight-or-flight situations.

Being late for a date or being afraid to speak in public often triggers our survival reflexes. It's up to all of us to train ourselves away from physical and behavioral overreactions—and breath is your tool. You can manage your anxiety by breathing with intention, focus, and concentration. Practice this breathing technique often, so that it becomes automatic. After all, what could be more natural than breathing?

Remember the NTB breath and you will always be stronger than your anxiety. Now that you *are* stronger than it, take what was negative—your nervous energy—and channel it in to positive, focused energy as you go after your goals and dreams. You got this—let's own it!

2

Smile More

MORE SMILES means less stress. And less stress means less anxiety.

That's what we need in our lives. And we *can* have it. We're so busy looking at what we don't have, why don't we look at what we *do* have for a change?

Here's one thing we all can give that costs nothing: a smile. No one is too poor to give a smile. No one is too rich to give a smile. And smiling diminishes anxiety. When we smile, we feel happier. A positive chemical reaction in the brain ignites. Serotonin flows through us, which reduces stress. The world looks brighter—a lot brighter. We create light inside and outside ourselves.

I've had dark moments when I wondered, "What's the point?" I'm sure you have, too. I've felt unfulfilled, like there's way too much emptiness to ever find happiness. I've also felt so stressed that I sweated and panicked and had a horrible breathless sensation, as though I'd lost something and would never find it. Do you know that feeling?

I've felt anxiety take over my heartbeat, send my blood coursing too fast through my nervous body, making me sick to my stomach. And too many times I've allowed nervousness to take over my face, setting my mouth into a tight line or a frown.

But I've also learned that smiling changes everything. Smiling creates light in the darkness. Smiling enables me to find happiness within myself. It calms the nerves within, lightens the load. It has the power to change my entire state of mind.

Try it right now. Put this book down for a second and smile. But hold on! I'm talking about a big, authentic smile. Even if your smile starts out a little fake, hang on to it until it becomes genuine. Here are a few pointers:

- Imagine your cheeks lifting your whole face up.
- Let the smile enter your eyes. Let the glow within shine through.
- Make sure that your lips aren't touching one another. Relax your mouth.
- Enjoy the feeling and let it spread warmth both inside and out.

If these tips don't work then just stick a pen between your teeth and hold it there and watch what happens! This is called the *pen test*. Believe it or not, in a lab setting, this test reduced the anxiety of everyone who tried it.

Science suggests that smiling during times of short-term stress may reduce the body's stress response, regardless of whether we're happy. Remember that you can smile anytime and anyplace. Just beware: It's contagious.

3

Sleep and Nap

AH, SLEEP! Yes, sleep. You are so vital to our lives, so important for owning anxiety and life in general. A few years back, I started to prioritize sleep and this did so much for me. I felt way clearer and less anxious, almost like I could handle more—more challenges, more surprises, more of the stuff that may have set my anxiety off before.

I was inspired by my father, who is an amazing sleeper.

My dad is seventy. He plays tennis three times a week, lifts weights, and does cardio regularly. He eats only a little junk food. He loves his wine and happily drinks a couple of glasses a few times a week. He still works quite a bit and through hard work has made an exceptional living for himself. He rarely gets sick and has no major health issues. He's very calm. Hardly ever does he have a really bad day or lose his cool. Basically, my dad is the opposite of anxious.

How does he do it? He naps. A lot. He takes one afternoon nap and usually falls asleep on the couch after dinner while watching TV. And is he shy about it? Definitely not!

I became a big napper because of my dad. I take one a day for fifteen to twenty minutes. And I love it. I excitedly set the timer on my phone then turn the device to silent, intentionally lie back on my couch, kick up my feet, and close my eyes. I focus on my breath, taking full, deep inhales and exhales. I let myself recharge. Even if I don't fall asleep, I go into an almost meditative state.

When the timer goes off, I feel refreshed, even if I haven't slept. I'm calmer and full of a relaxed peace that overtakes my entire being. There's no anxiety after napping. This is what it's all about; this is why I nap.

Want to own your anxiety? Close your eyes and nap more often.

And want to sleep better, faster, and easier at bedtime? Follow this advice:

Plan a wind-down time. Give yourself thirty minutes of screen-free chill time before bed. Relax, mentally and physically. Read something soothing, meditate, write in your journal, or do whatever—do you, but the relaxed you.

Put away your phone. Our smartphones might be an incredible addition to our lives, but they also arguably give us more anxiety than anything else. Stay off yours for thirty minutes before bed.

Avoid social media. Don't think that I'm going to let you get away with using social media on your computer or tablet either! No social media for at least thirty minutes before bed.

Avoid eating and drinking. I strongly encourage you not to eat or drink for two or three hours before bed. This short fast will allow your body to rest while you're asleep. It will lead to a smoother duration of zzz's and fewer bathroom breaks.

4

Swim

I'VE BEEN anxious, stressed, and depressed before jumping in, but once I hit the water and let myself sink, time stops and my mental stresses temporarily fade away. I'm at peace. There's silence, except for my breath, which I mindfully own, stillness, except for my movement. There's space. And serenity. Swimming gives me all this, plus one badass muscle-building and defining practice that is part workout and part meditation.

Whether in a public pool, at the gym, in a backyard pool with friends, or in the ocean or a lake, swimming offers several practical benefits, including reducing anxiety. Does anyone reading this actually feel worse after they get out of the water? Unless you can't swim or have a bad association with water, you probably feel invigorated and calm after you hop out.

That's because "vigorous exercise like swimming can significantly decrease both anxiety and depression," says sports psychologist Aimee C. Kimball, director of mental training at the Center for Sports Medicine at University of Pittsburgh Medical Center.

But there's more. While swimming offers major mental health benefits and releases endorphins, it is believed that all moderate exercise can promote the creation of new neurons in the brain.

On top of all this, swimming can produce a calming, meditative flow similar to that of traditional meditation practices and relaxed yoga. Breath after breath, stroke after stroke. This predictable precision of movement coupled with deep, intentional breathing helps to quell anxiety.

Swimming has more to offer than getting a "swimmer's body." Clearly, developing a "swimmers mind" wouldn't be a bad thing either.

• • •

#OwnYourAnxiety tip: If swimming isn't your thing, try the new float trend people are loving, soak up a warm bath in your tub (more on this in tip 18 "Take Warm Showers or Baths"), hop in the steam room or sauna at your gym, or just dance in the rain with a big smile on your face!

5

Quit or Reduce Coffee

I DON'T ACTUALLY like this tip, because I *love* coffee. I love the comforting aroma that wraps all around you when you step into a good coffee shop. I love the taste, those sweet, tart notes. I love the ritual. And I love that just as soon as you drink it, you feel something warm, energy-boosting, and decadent rush through your body. It's no wonder that a huge portion of the world wakes up and wants their morning coffee. I totally get it. Yet I'm consistently amazed by how many people complain about their anxiety issues and still drink coffee.

The major issue with coffee and anxiety is the caffeine. It's even referred to as a psychoactive drug, which ScienceDaily defines as "a chemical substance that acts primarily upon the central nervous system, where it alters brain function, resulting in temporary changes in perception, mood, consciousness, and behavior." Sources say that caffeine is the world's most commonly used psychoactive drug. Yikes.

Caffeine is not the innocuous wake-up drink we think it is. The American Psychiatric Association named four caffeine-related syndromes: caffeine-intoxication, caffeine-induced

Eliminating coffee can be an incredibly powerful shift for owning the energy of anxiety.

· · · · · · · · · ·

anxiety disorder, caffeine-induced sleep disorder, and caffeine-related disorder not otherwise specified.

Caffeine is fuel to anxiety.

Cause for concern? I'd say, yes. "But I love my coffee!" you're thinking as you shake this book in your hands. (Is that the caffeine talking, or are you resisting this advice?) Ask yourself this: What do you love more, your cup of caffeine or yourself?

It's a hard choice, and I'll admit there have been times in my life when I chose coffee. That didn't work out so well, though. And that's why I stopped drinking it for eight months. When I finally gave in and had a cup, I thought I was having a seriously massive anxiety attack. My heart started beating fast, my hands were shaking, my pits sweating. Then came that annoying eye twitch. It felt like I would blast out of my chair! This made me realize just what a huge impact coffee has on my day-to-day anxiety. I did some online digging, and it turns out that many anxiety-prone people experience a strong reaction to caffeine. I mean, it makes sense. A lot of sense.

Why?

For one reason, caffeine is a stimulant. Stimulants give us a jolt, a shock, a burst of energy. We, the anxious, don't need any of that because we already feel wired for no good reason. Adding a stimulant is like tossing propane on an already blazing fire. It just gets bigger.

And secondly, one study showed caffeine may change activity in the amygdala, an important part of our brain that's responsible for how we respond to and measure fear. The amygdala determines if we go into a fight-or-flight state in response to a threat. So, when an environmental stimulus provokes stress and anxiety, our amygdala decides whether to fight or to run, so to speak. It's no wonder that the coffee habit is wreaking havoc on our anxiety-consumed generation.

If you're anxiety prone, I highly suggest cutting back on your coffee intake. You can even do this in steps so that it's not quite so overwhelming.

Step 1: If you drink two or more cups of coffee a day, start by reducing to one a day.

Step 2: If you have one coffee a day, try decaf for a few weeks.

Step 3: Once you've mastered decaf, try replacing coffee with a delicious herbal, caffeine-free tea.

Step 4: Keep this up. The aim is to be caffeine-free for at least one to six months and then to observe the impact this change has on your anxiety. That's the goal, and take it seriously.

Still with me? If you're going to try this method, great! If you're trying it and you've been caffeine-free for a month, that's amazing! How are your anxiety levels now? Notice any differences?

Nobody says that positive change is easy, but we know that it leads to positive growth. Cutting back on or eliminating coffee can be an incredibly powerful shift for owning the energy of anxiety.

6

Drink Herbal Tea

WHEN I was in my early twenties, I lived in San Francisco and worked in Silicon Valley for an amazing start-up company. The CEO and founder, Suneet, was someone I looked up to. He had this way of exercising composed analytical thought, especially in high-pressure situations. It was inspiring.

In the afternoon, while I was desperate for my second or third cup of coffee, Suneet would fix himself a cup of herbal tea. He'd sip from that cup for the rest of the day, while orchestrating his business moves step by consistent step, bringing his dream ever closer to reality. I would look at him with that tea and think, *This guy is calm and in control. He doesn't need coffee to stay engaged and alert. His focus is perennial. And it's on the inside.*

Largely inspired by Suneet, I replaced coffee with herbal tea. Whenever I say no to the temptation of a large coffee or double espresso (my old go-to), I remember him. I think about how, as he led, he maintained an intense drive *and* inner peace. Now, I don't suffer the highs and lows of caffeine addiction.

The first sip of a steaming cup of tea is therapeutic.

• • • • • • • • • •

Now, that first sip of a steaming, warm cup of tea is therapeutic. It took some time to get here, but here I am! I really enjoy tea.

If you're like I was as a coffee drinker, you may not know about the various herbal teas out there waiting to be discovered. These light, clean, and refreshing drinks are made of a mixture of leaves, flowers, seeds, roots, and/or bark, their flavors extracted when you add hot water. Herbal teas can be a potent holistic remedy full of benefits that will help you not only temper anxiety but be a healthier person all around.

There are so many known benefits to herbal teas:

• To state the obvious, they're not full of anxiety-inducing caffeine!

• They're hydrating (as opposed to having the diuretic properties of excess coffee).

- They soothe achy cold and flu symptoms. The less sick we feel, the less anxiety we'll experience because we won't be inhibited from going after what we want. Try teas with ginger, rosehip, chamomile, or hibiscus when you're feeling under the weather.

- They're stress busting. Specific herbal teas, such as chamomile and lemon balm, are linked to stress reduction.

- They relieve nausea. Ginger tea can reduce nausea and calm an upset stomach.

- They induce sleep. Drinking lavender tea, one of my personal favorites, is a relaxing pre-sleep ritual for me. I love to sip it and put lavender oil into my diffuser to help me get a great rest.

- They have other specific health benefits. Tulsi, or holy basil, tea, for instance, is used as a natural remedy for anxiety. It is also thought to enhance the reproductive, central nervous, cardiovascular, and gastric systems. It has been said that it combats acne and even fights cancer.

Get into the herbal tea phenomenon. Enjoy the flavor, find your preferred brands, and learn about the health benefits. Practice a bit of self-love with every sip you take. The simple ritual of sipping tea can be an exceptionally chill way to de-stress and relax. Make this your ritual. Who's down for some tea time?

Quit or Reduce Alcohol

S O YOU enjoy a nice bottle of wine? Me too. You enjoy a
well-crafted cocktail or four? Me too. You enjoy a few cold
beers on a hot day? Me too. You enjoy alcohol. We're not
hooked, but yes, me too.

When I was fourteen years old, I started throwing parties at
nightclubs. I learned how to drink before that, on a family trip
to Mexico, where if you could see over the bar, you'd be served.
I've been having "fun" with alcohol for a long, long time.

I've used it to chill out and relax. I've used it to wind up for
a night out. I've used it to get into a more romantic mood. I've
used it to make me freer and more fun in social situations and
to make the company of those I really didn't vibe with a bit
more tolerable.

Sound familiar?

So many of us use booze to help us mask our internal
issues, fears, and hang-ups rather than dealing with them.
Instead of going to the root of the issue, we slap a liquid solution onto the problem. But this not only takes you further
away from your awesome, exceptional self; it can also make

When you cut back on or quit alcohol you will find that you're clearer, healthier, and less anxious.

. . . .

you terribly anxious, when you could have avoided a bout of anxiety altogether.

Countless negative side effects accompany alcohol consumption. I know I've tried to justify my consumption as "moderate" drinking, but that is often a self-delusion. Let's get real about what "moderate" means. It's about half a glass of wine—and I don't mean half a glass of what's generally poured these days. I mean two to three ounces. By this metric, when I was still drinking "moderately," I would have been considered an alcoholic ten times over! I'm sure a lot of you would, too!

Alcohol changes our levels of serotonin and other neurotransmitters; it is linked to increased levels of anxiety. And it's not just the chemical effects of alcohol that hurt. Drinking a lot tends to negatively impact other parts of our lives, too. When we drink more, we generally sleep worse. Then we medicate hangovers and boost our energy with coffee. We eat crappy food for the carb kick and we work out less—or at least way less intensely—because our bodies are drained.

This tip kind of sucks, right? Tough to handle since drinking is a major part of life in our society, yeah? Hold on. Perhaps it doesn't suck. Let's look at this from a different perspective. Maybe it's a great thing to realize that choosing a life with little to no alcohol is one of the best things you can do for yourself. You're not holding this book because you're interested in being a prisoner of anxiety. You don't want to just scrape by. You're here with me because you want an incredible, inspiring, fulfilled, healthy life. That's our birthright, so let's live it.

What do you want more—that boozy night out, that bottle of wine and round(s) of tequila shots, leading to regrets and a hangover, or an anxiety-owned, vibrant you, feeling strong, clear, and confident in who you are?

Which will it be?

I'll never forget when I decided to host my first all-day seminar. In the past, I had been hired for various talks; but at this one, I was doing about 75 percent of the speaking and I was in charge of organizing the entire event! Worse, I had only about four weeks to prepare. I could feel the anxiety rising ferociously inside me.

I decided that the only way to succeed was by cutting out alcohol completely, because that meant no partying, no wasted time, no hangovers, and no sickness. My birthday happened during that time, and I went to my party with bells on, but I stuck with club soda and lime. Like a boss.

Guess what? The seminar was hugely successful and, looking back, it helped me realize what a negative impact drinking had on my life. It robbed me of time and health. It connected me with the wrong people. It fueled my anxiety.

When we own our lives, we create our futures. When you cut back on or quit alcohol not only will you find that you're clearer, healthier, and less anxious, but you'll also rid yourself of those brutal "morning after" (or next few days or longer) shame spirals where you don't know what you did the night before. Plus the dehydration from drinking really affects anxiety in a mean way.

There you have it. I've spelled it out! So, now, the questions to ask yourself are how will you reach your goals, and what kind of life do you see yourself living? There's a huge link between alcohol and anxiety. How big is up to you.

8

Quit Drugs

RUGS MIGHT be among the worst triggers of anxiety, and by giving them up, you will do much to own your anxiety. How do you feel after a night of partying? Coke, MDMA, E, pot, you name it. As you come down from the high, do you feel depressed, anxious, easily agitated?

Some of my worst anxiety attacks happened after an intense night of partying. I remember lying in bed, trying to fall asleep but hearing only my heart racing. On the way to work, I'd feel anxious, stressed. I'd sweat for no reason. These were the aftereffects of the garbage in my system.

How many times have you promised to quit partying? If you're like me, too many times to count. But I've stopped because I feel the positive results of not partying: I'm higher-functioning, clearer about my goals, mentally and physically fitter, less agitated, closer with the people I love most, and healthier. Don't beat yourself up if you're not there yet, but know that you can and will be. Something great is waiting for you: the incomparable high of living a more evolved, disciplined life.

9

Hug and Cuddle More

THIS WORLD needs more hugging and less rushing. You and I do, too. I'm often that person who responds to an outstretched hand with two wide-open arms and by saying, "Bring it in here. I'm a hugger." Yes, that's me. I admit it. There are times when, for all kinds of reasons, I decide to hold back on my hug instinct. And can I be honest with you? I usually regret it. Hugging is such a wondrous, feel-good gesture. Plus it helps to break the ice and even makes people laugh.

If hugging were mandatory for greetings between all world leaders, there'd be a lot less war, don't you think? Although it's probably tough to make hugging a new international law, we can make it happen more in our personal lives. The benefits to relieving anxiety are proven in a big way.

For those eager to give and receive them, hugs have many benefits. First, there's the anecdotal evidence: Do you ever feel worse after a big, juicy hug? I highly doubt it. Also, hugging releases oxytocin. So when we give and receive a hug or engage in an awesome cuddle session—and yes, this happens during sex, too—this super-cool "love hormone" is released.

Oxytocin is known to have a considerable effect on our cardio-vascular system and lessens anxiety and stress. It can slow our heart rate and lower blood pressure, increase immunity and reduce pain. Some studies even show that intravenous administration of oxytocin to women in labor decreases blood loss and regulates blood pressure.

So here's my question for you: How can you incorporate more hugs and cuddles into your life? I'm not suggesting you hug perfect strangers, but you might think of some close friends and family members to hug more often and for a little bit longer when you say hello and goodbye. And what about cuddling? If you have someone who you're intimate with, don't be afraid to cuddle more. Enjoy it.

•   •   •

#OwnYourAnxiety tip: If being hugged by a stranger makes you feel anxious, that's okay. Honor how you feel. Maybe a handshake or a smile is your comfortable, warm greeting. That's great!

Another word of caution: Be sensitive to others. If you're not sure that the person you're greeting wants to be hugged, don't do it. Be mindful and respectful of the feelings and personal boundaries of others.

10

Once a Day, Eat in Peace

MEALTIME CAN be meditative. It offers a time to slow down, breathe mindfully, check in with ourselves, give gratitude and thanks for the food we're about to consume, and take a break from professional pressures. Yet so few people remember to treat meals this way.

Do you find that, when you sit down to eat, you focus on your food or on something else, such as your phone, your computer, the TV, or entertaining the person/people sitting with you?

Trust me, I feel you. I used to eat with my phone in one hand, my computer in front of me, and other people all around, generally at the office. I was a multitasking machine—working, learning something, or connecting with others but not mindfully eating my food! I totally missed out on the opportunity that meals offer: a chance to stop and re-center. When we're not focused on enjoying our meals, we lose what could be a meditative, special, and calming break from the stressors of the day.

When we're distracted, eating goes from being a simple, pleasurable task to a possible anxiety trigger that can spiral.

Let's say that you're eating lunch at your desk with colleagues at theirs all around you. You're checking emails as you take a bite of your sandwich. You hear the ding notifying you that a new email just came through, so you scroll to the top, open it up, and promptly feel anxiety-provoking butterflies in your stomach. You swallow your food and try to concentrate on the email. Once you've recovered from this little episode, you have another bite. Now, mid-chew, your phone rings. You quickly swallow and say, "Hello?" It's an aggravating call center telling you that you owe money for something, or it's your sick parent, needy sibling, or psycho client. Once again, your breathing stops, and then it starts faster than before. When the call is over, it's time for your last bite (if you still have an appetite), but your boss walks up to your desk and asks for something that's due today, which you totally forgot to do; or an employee approaches asking if he can have another one-on-one, please.

And now, your lunch is ruined. You either wolf down the rest without even tasting it or you can't put another bite into your nervous stomach. Fast-forward thirty minutes. "Why is my stomach making noises? Why am I feeling a little bit nauseous?"

Do you see how the anxiety spiral happened here? By robbing ourselves of a meal and a break, we enter the anxiety spiral. This used to happen to me way too often. But I had no idea. I hope that by reading this example, you're able to become more conscious and modify your life.

My invitation to you is to make a different choice about how you eat. Reserve one meal per day for yourself. Make a date with you! And enjoy it. That's hot. Eat something you love for the taste or for the healing impact it has on your body. Think about this as you slowly chew your food. Savor this sacred time as you nourish yourself with the gifts of the earth.

Get a Massage

MASSAGE CAN sort you out and calm you down. It's so therapeutic. It offers tons of physical benefits, such as reducing cortisol levels and muscle tension, and mental benefits that include lowering anxiety. In a recent randomized study that tested the effects of traditional Swedish massage versus light therapy on patients with Generalized Anxiety Disorder (GAD), the group that received two forty-five-minute massages per week reported reduced anxiety more often than those who received light therapy.

Massage can boost the immune system and lead to better sleep, two key factors in better mental health. Because of the oxytocin that gets released, human-to-human touch has big health benefits.

Whenever I feel stressed and anxious, massage proves to be therapeutic. A five-minute walk away from my old office, there was an amazing spa. Often, I would book a massage as the day was winding down. Looking back, I chuckle to recall how fully anxious I felt when leaving work early. Self-love was a foreign concept to me then. I would send as many emails as I could before taking off, not telling my staff that I was going for a massage and hoping not to be seen as I walked to the spa. Even while I undressed, I hastily checked my cell phone before putting it on silent. Finally, when I closed the locker door, I felt a wave of relaxing energy flood over me. Well, most of the time. Once, though, I made the mistake of bringing my phone to the massage table with me, which completely ruined the experience. The massage therapist thought I was a total type A nutjob. That part was funny, too.

"It's your time and your money," she said.

Don't make the same mistake I made!

When we channel our anxiety into positive, contained energy, we're better able to feel, think, and do. You might enjoy your massage even more than someone who isn't anxious in the first place because you're getting a high level of relief. I know I do.

Here are a few tips, for home or at the spa, for getting the most out of a massage and incorporating it into your holistic wellness regimen:

- Use the nose-to-belly (NTB) breathing technique from the first tip in the book. Correlating your breath with a massage takes it to another, heightened, level and adds *even more* relaxation.

- If certain scents calm you, use an essential oil of your choice during a massage. You might even use a vaporizer in the room so that the scent envelops you.

- Massage yourself. That's right. You can massage your own hands, arms, neck, scalp, legs, and any other part. When you feel anxiety coming on, you might try touching the spot where you feel it most—your forehead, your eyes, your neck—and asking your body to relax.

12

Chew Slower

D o you chew your food mindfully or do you inhale it? There are a lot of inhalers these days. We're always rushing. I mean, why slow down to eat, right? Wrong.

When we chew quickly, we're far from relaxed. When we chew slowly, we slow down.

When I'm having a meal, I usually, instinctively take the first few bites quickly and chew super-fast—unless I mindfully approach the meal with the intention of savoring it. Going in mindfully changes everything about our relationship with food, and it also holds true that mindfulness changes everything about our lives. Choose any situation and approach it mindfully—you'll always end up in a better place.

Aside from the known benefits—such as better digestion, increased weight loss, and enjoyment—chewing slowly transforms your meal from a mundane, rushed chore into a higher spiritual privilege. How we chew can determine how we experience our entire meal. When we rush, we're the opposite of anxiety-free: we're anxiety-laden. Deliberate, thoughtful movement is how we find our center and practice savoring the moment. What better example of savoring a moment than enjoying our food? Appreciating happens when chewing slows down. There's a direct correlation.

Chew slower when you're eating by yourself and when you're eating with others. There's another side benefit to the "slow food movement": life always seems to hurry by, and this is your chance to alter time and find pleasure in it. They're a blessing, really—food and the moment.

Here's how to eat mindfully:

- After each bite, put your utensils (or hands) down.

- Pick your utensils up again only after you've swallowed your bite of food.

- While you're chewing, focus on the flavor sensations. Imagine getting closer to them by using your imagination and your mind, the way you would on a wine-tasting adventure.

Is this going to make meal times longer? Yes! You might take a few minutes longer to eat, you might be OOO (out of office) for a few extra minutes at lunchtime, but calming your anxiety and taking back the flavor of life is worth every single bite.

13

Drink More Water

DRINK A lot of water. Even before I became an advisor and minority owner of Flow (the mindfully positive alkaline water in a recyclable box), I was drinking more than eight glasses a day.

I love water. I find it so purifying and cleansing. It does wonders for spiking my energy and managing my hunger. In fact, on days when I'm not drinking enough water, I'm more sluggish and hungrier than on days when I drink more.

Our brains are mostly water. They crave good hydration, which helps us stay focused, energized, and alert. From a weight-management standpoint, water helps reduce the amount we eat by filling us up with a calorie-free, clean substance. Water speeds up our metabolism and flushes toxins from our bodies.

We all know water is great for us. But did you know it can have a major impact on our mental health? Staying hydrated can ease anxiety.

When our bodies are dehydrated, our cells feel it at a molecular level and send signals that there's an underlying threat to our survival. Being thirsty means really bad news. There's reason to believe being thirsty may cause anxiety.

Have you ever felt your anxiety increase after a night of drinking? The symptoms of a hangover are caused by major dehydration brought on by alcohol consumption. Might it be possible that the increased feelings of shame, fear, and agitation that accompany hangovers at least partially stem from the body feeling threatened by dehydration?

Here's something else you need to know about dehydration: It commonly results in mood changes. Why? Because a lack of good liquid in the body limits blood flow to the brain. Feeling thirsty? Good! Here are some quick tips to increase your water consumption:

- First thing in the morning, drink two large glasses of water—that's one liter. We wake up dehydrated, so hydrating ourselves first thing is important. Plus, if being dehydrated is linked to negative moods, maybe there's a correlation between your "not being a morning person" and not drinking enough water early in the day.

- Drink another glass before you eat breakfast, lunch, and dinner.

- When you feel hungry for that late-afternoon or late-night snack, drink another glass of water first.

- Drink another glass or two throughout the day. Keep water with you, by your desk, in your bag, in your car.

If you follow these tips, you'll be consuming a great amount of clean liquid per day and you'll be on your way to owning your anxiety. Raise your good, clean, refreshing water with me right now. Cheers!

14

Don't Walk Alone at Night if It Scares You

ONCE LEFT a late-night function in a city that isn't my own. I love to walk so didn't think much about the thirty-minute stroll back to the hotel. I had a good sense of the way. But, being new to the city, I took a wrong turn. Before I knew it, the buildings looked run-down and rough people on the streets stared me down in that way that said I should get out, fast. My fight-or-flight reflex kicked in. I went from taking long, mindful breaths to short, quick ones. I became anxious and hot.

As if the universe knew I needed an intervention, a yellow cab slowly drove toward me. I flagged it down and hopped inside. Everything was fine.

Was my walk worth it? It definitely was not. I didn't think everything through, then placed myself in harm's way, and my anxiety went sky-high.

To own anxiety, we need to be mindful, protect ourselves, and be safe. Things that can potentially trigger anxiety attacks must be avoided; risks need to be assessed and good choices made. Walk proudly. Walk safely. Walk mindfully.

15

Play

CAN I TELL you something honestly? Not too long ago, I realized that I was spending way too much time focused on "being an adult." I was too focused on what life is supposed to look like "at my age." So what happens if we don't fit the standard? Catastrophe? Major issues? Life is going to suck? Of course not!

One of the best ways to combat the pressures of the adult world is to play! We need to play more. Why? Because when we play, we forget. When we play, we escape. When we play, we own anxiety, because we shift our energy into something creative and anxiety pretty much stops showing up.

Being more playful is an attitude and an intentional way of acting that is available for all to embrace. Recently, I was at a family barbecue and my anxiety was on high. Suddenly, my niece, Romi, ran up to me and wanted me to play outside with her. She asked about five times, and then reluctantly (because it required that I get out of my own way) I accepted the offer. (Pro tip: The hardest *way* to get out of is *your own way*.)

The hardest way to get out of is your own.

· · · · · · · · · ·

Outside, this adorable three-year-old and I entered a world of unknowns . . . the soccer ball or the oversized baseball and bat? The grass or the mud? Dance like a ballerina or do yoga? Endless options, not enough time. Instead of embracing the grown-up way of playing, I just joined hers. *I played.* Dammit, I played *well*. And she played even better than me. She played like a pro. And I sure as heck owned my anxiety.

While playing, I got out of my own head,
owned my anxiety, and felt happier to be alive.

My friends with children tell me that when they play with their kids, they feel purposeful, connected, humbled, and grateful. One friend told me that he feels more at ease when playing with his kids than when doing anything else. And it doesn't end with children. This same strategy for owning anxiety applies to playing with animals.

Is there anything cuter and more relaxing than watching adorable pet videos on YouTube? What's more relaxing than playing with a super-cute puppy? Or watching animals at the zoo? The other day, while awaiting news about my mother, who is going through cancer treatments, I felt anxious and sort of mentally dark, so I googled a YouTube video called "Cute Animals Cuddling," which was a mashup of different types of animals—from cats to owls to hamsters to a baby racoon—getting cuddled by their humans and loving it. This simple little video was incredibly therapeutic and a major anxiety reliever for me. I've even been known to watch dogs play in the park. The way their tails wag, how they sniff absolutely everything, their bond with their owners, how they bark at other dogs (what are they saying to each other?), and their simple, upbeat way of life always makes me smile and chill out.

And it seems I'm not alone in that. Animals do wonders for us in the pursuit of stress relief. According to an article by Steven Feldman on the Anxiety and Depression Association of America website, 74 percent of pet owners reported mental health improvements from pet ownership, and 75 percent of friends or family members of pet owners reported that their friend or family member's mental health improved from pet ownership. This is what Feldman calls the *pet effect*.

Human-animal interactions, or HAI for short, have been proven to release oxytocin, or the "love hormone," into the body. Oxytocin boosts mental health and reduces anxiety and stress. There are many things that naturally increase oxytocin, such as hugging, cuddling (with people), and yes, sex (see tip 9). It's also released just by petting a dog or a cat.

Pets and other animals are a serious gift to humans. And, if you're like me and currently have a schedule that isn't right for pet ownership, you can still receive some of the benefits by visiting the dog park or a cat café or the zoo—or even by watching some cute animal clips online. Want to take it a step further and do a good deed while managing your anxiety? Contact your local animal shelter about volunteering. Imagine how awesome that could be.

So next time you see a lil pup or senior dog cruising by, don't be shy. Ask the owner if you can give the four-legged friend a pat. It'll do wonders for you and, who knows, maybe it'll reduce Fido's anxiety, too. And, if there's no Fido around, hop online and start watching your favorite animals do their thing. Let's also not forget, next time a child wants to play, play!

16

Sing Out Loud

THEY SAY music is the speech of angels. Although I agree that song is angelic, we've all heard singers who don't sound so heavenly. I, for instance, am an okay rapper (true story), but can I sing? Not a chance. I'm awful. But guess what? It doesn't matter! Why? Because it feels good and it *does you good* to sing. And that's why I sing.

Many studies have looked at the impact of singing on human health. Researchers from the University of East Anglia found that people who took part in a community singing group maintained or improved their mental health. The combination of singing and socializing promoted an ongoing feeling of belonging and well-being.

Professor Tom Shakespeare also studied choral singing groups and found that even when there was no planned end goal—such as a big performance—choir members reported that singing helped them feel happy and taught them how to have fun in a social environment. For many people, social environments spark anxiety. But like anything, the more we do it, the easier it becomes.

Research has shown that choir singing (and even listening to a choir) lowers our stress hormones, which in turn makes us feel a sense of well-being—and decreases anxiety.

So belt it out in the shower, behind the wheel, at the karaoke bar, or as you whip up a meal. And sing with others, too. I want to hear you roar, my friend. It's not about how angelic you sound but about sharing the joy of singing and enjoying the moment.

Let's just say public singing isn't your thing. Don't stress it! Singing still has major benefits, with or without a group around to hear how bad—I mean how good—you are.

Singing stimulates the vagus nerve. It's part of our parasympathetic nervous system and helps us activate the relaxation response.

And guess what? Reports say that the louder the better when it comes to activating the vagus nerve.

So next time you're feeling anxious, sing! Whether or not we sound like angels is beside the point, really; what matters is that we do it. That's how we'll own anxiety.

17

Get "Scentual"

I'VE ALWAYS been deeply affected by scents. When I was a young teen, I was the first of my friends to become interested in colognes and fragrances. I'd find myself scratching the fragrance inserts of magazines over and over, transported by the amazing smells that reminded me of faraway places and exotic destinations. I spent my hard-earned allowance and money from my part-time job on all kinds of colognes, more for myself than to impress anyone else with how good I smelled. Call me "smellfish." (Bad joke.)

These days, I'm much more attuned to natural scents and oils rather than synthetic fragrances. I select scents based on the positive effects they have on my mood. And oils and other scents *can* help you manage your anxiety. "Scent has been found to attenuate the effects of the hormone activity that create anxious feelings in the limbic region of the brain, as well as boost levels of hormones known to lift the mood. Essential oils are useful, efficient tools to shift these fearful sensations and mindset on a daily basis," my colleague Elena Brower shared with me. In fact, pleasing scents have been used to reduce anxiety in cancer patients receiving treatments as well. Knowing this information is an essential and easy tool to keep with you as you own your anxiety. They're used in dentist offices to lower people's stress levels during checkups and procedures, too.

As I write this, I have my lavender essential oil gently diffusing beside me. Compared with how I felt before I sat down to write, I can say without doubt that I'm calmer and more relaxed, all with a little olfactory help. This is a really easy tip to help you find a sense of inner serenity. Why not treat yourself? It only makes "scents."

• • •

#OwnYourAnxiety tip: Anxiety bosses know that spending money on things that will help us become our best selves makes a lot of "scents." (Wow, this word is fun to play with!) Invest in diffusers, oils, candles, and soaps, knowing that the research backs up the calming effects of certain aromas. Rosewater, lavender, bergamot, and chamomile all have been proven to reduce anxiety.

18

Take Warm
Showers or Baths

WATER NOT only has cleansing properties, it also has healing properties. Human beings throughout time have used water therapeutically, to calm down, re-center, and relax. From Ancient Greece to the Roman and Ottoman Empires to ancient Buddhists in India, water has provided relief and calm.

And this isn't just to do with physically cleansing; it has been used in ritualistic and spiritual cleanses, too. There must be a reason that our sages have long embraced the power of H_2O.

Years ago, when I was a "type A entrepreneur" and at the height of my anxiety spiral, I took cold showers a lot. I was exhausted all the time, and cold showers helped me wake up. But they also jolted my system and robbed me of the simple pleasure of warm, steamy showers because I wanted them to end as quickly as possible!

When I learned that my cold-shower habit was inducing my anxiety, I made the change. And now, I love every moment of it. The warm steam rising, those comforting beads of water landing on my skin, and that feeling of being drenched in the liquid heat is so soothing. What could be better? Warm showers are linked to that great "love hormone" we've talked about before—oxytocin.

To build on the previous tip, "Get 'Scentual,'" go on an adventure in which you intentionally set out to explore what anxiety-owning scents are your faves, and buy them so that you forever transform your experience of showering. Remember that rosewater, lavender, bergamot, and chamomile have all been proven to reduce anxiety.

The next time you step foot in your shower, take a centering breath and consciously remind yourself that the simple act of showering is an opportunity to own your anxiety. Every warm bead falling on your skin is an invitation to connect to a refreshing new way to look at your anxiety. Find a centering calm as the water splashes on you and an inspiring hope as you accept the possibility that what you're doing not only feels good physically, it is enhancing you mentally.

Let's turn the faucet to warm. Let that calming steam fill the air and a new relationship with anxiety fill up your life.

19

Wear Comfy Clothes

SOCIETY PLACES a lot of pressure on us to always look our best. From our hair to our weight to how our skin looks to whether there are bags under our eyes to what we're wearing, we're shamed into feeling that if we don't look like supermodels all the time, we're not good enough (an anxiety causer for sure). This tip is about being authentically yourself and feeling comfortable. And a good starting point for this is the clothes that we wear. What happens if you ignore all that pressure and decide to dress only for your own enjoyment? What if your work outfits, your dance shoes, your pants weren't about looking like you just stepped off a runway but about physical comfort? Keep in mind, I'm not suggesting that we all wear onesies. I don't own one myself (yet!)—let's just clear that up. What I *am* suggesting is that the obsession with fashion and perfect aesthetics may come at a high price: your mental health.

Whenever I'm feeling anxious, one of the first things I do is put on some super-comfy clothes. I love it when my loose sweatpants create a cozy, warm, and safe bubble around my legs. I love my warm Bombas socks and snug slippers. I love cushy hoodies with lots of room in the shoulders. Sometimes, especially if it's cold out, I even love to wear a soft toque or beanie. Put it all together and it's my anti-anxiety outfit. When I'm wearing it, it gives me that warm, secure feeling that helps me re-center and ground myself. From that place, I can focus on what's causing my anxiety, and from there, I can own it.

What's your anti-anxiety outfit? What perfectly comfortable clothes make you feel warm, snug, and safe?

The next time you're feeling out of sorts, make a costume change. Get out of those tight pants. No more itchy collars and stiff seams. Once you change into your anti-anxiety clothes, I bet you'll feel way better. You'll find that being physically loose, cozy, and relaxed might result in your mood taking on the same qualities. On a muscular level, when we're in our comfy gear, there's room for relaxation.

Let yourself occupy your comfy clothes and relax right into them. By making this little ritual a special treat, you're training yourself to favor relaxation over tension. So the next time you have an anxiety episode, try changing your outfit to change your state of mind. That's something we can all feel comfortable about.

•   •   •

#OwnYourAnxiety tip: If you can't stay home and get your comfiest self on, wear the cushiest version of your work gear to the office. Let yourself feel grateful and cozy, as you know you're honoring *you* while crushing life!

20

Move Your Body

LOVE TO move. I love to exercise. It's such a gift to have a body. It's a privilege. From a spiritual perspective, many believe that our bodies are "on loan" to us for this lifetime. Why not enjoy them? Moving them isn't about how big your muscles are or how sleek your abs are. It's about being grateful and present to have a body to move. It's about embracing and knowing that as we move, we own anxiety. Let's invert any superficial paradigms that exist around how the body should look and instead make our new reality one of joyful movement.

Recently, my mother was having some bad side effects from her chemotherapy treatments. It was Mother's Day and our plan was that I would go to her apartment to hang out for a relaxing afternoon. We would order in a casual dinner from our favorite Middle Eastern restaurant and eat it while watching one of her best-loved movies. Conveniently, this Mother's Day fell on an absolutely beautiful Sunday.

Chemo takes its toll on the body. One of the side effects is weak muscles. My mother was in a lot of pain, but she wanted

Regular exercise
and movement
helps us become
comfortable
with our anxious
feelings.
· · · · · · · · ·

to get outside, as it had been several days since she'd been out. I give her so much credit because she found the strength to get herself together, put on her wig, and take a short walk with me outside.

As she began to move, she came back to life. Despite the pain, the presence of basic movement felt so soothing to her. We walked in a grassy field near her apartment, but amazingly, she decided that wasn't enough.

She said, "Let's go to the outdoor track," referring to a beautiful piece of property at a nearby school. So off we went.

When we arrived, mom held on to my arm, noticing the life all around us: a mother and daughter playing basketball, a soccer team practicing, an elderly couple going for a walk in the vegetable garden. We watched the people, perfect strangers in the heart of the city, all enjoying the weather and the day. I was so proud of how far she'd come.

Then, I noticed something. A man in his eighties, cane in hand, was slowly making his way around the track. "Mom, look at this man."

As she observed him round the bend, her jaw suddenly dropped and she said, "Wait a second. That's Dr. Friedman!"

He was her childhood doctor. They made eye contact, and the man approached. "It's so nice to see you!" my mother said.

"And you!" he replied.

It turns out, he was walking off the remnants of a major surgery. My mom shared that she had also undergone medical treatment and was doing her best to stay mobile.

"Good for you," he said. "Sitting inside all day feeling sorry for yourself only makes things worse. The biggest thing that we need to worry about isn't the cancer or whatever other illness we're facing, it's that thing between our ears. You have to move my dear, you have to move."

That encounter had a positive impact on my mother, but it also had a positive impact on me. When I'm feeling down or lethargic, I think of Dr. Friedman's words, and that gets me going again.

It's a well-known fact that moving our bodies helps us manage anxiety. Regular exercise and movement help us anxiety-prone types adjust to and eventually become comfortable with our fight-or-flight feelings. We can channel our energy into productive movement. This results in a decrease in cortisol levels.

Other benefits of movement and exercise include controlling our weight and reducing our risk of cardiovascular disease, type 2 diabetes, metabolic syndrome, and even some common cancers. Exercising also strengthens bones and muscles, which is why it helps us age better.

Exercise also feels similar to an anxiety attack—sweatiness, heart thumping, dry-mouth. When we exercise, it helps us get more comfortable with the symptoms we feel when anxious.

There are so many fun and inspiring ways to move. The trick is to find a way that works for you, one that you love or at least enjoy.

Physical activity isn't just a great way to own anxiety; it can also be effective in preventing it altogether.

21

Dance

I'LL BE honest. I'm not a good dancer. When the powers that be were deciding which skills to give out, they definitely skipped right over me in the dance department. Yet I often find myself dancing around my home. Or awkwardly moving to music when I'm out in the world. It doesn't matter that I don't move like Carlton from *The Fresh Prince of Bel-Air*, Beyoncé, or JT. Whatever. Ask anyone who enjoys dancing or who has ever danced and they'll tell you the same thing: Dancing makes them feel better. They'll also say the trick is to "dance like nobody is watching."

Dancing reduces anxiety in big, beautiful ways. It effectively combines two anxiety- and stress-reducing activities—music appreciation *and* exercise—into one wicked activity. It's no wonder that so many people, from young children to elderly folks, love to shake it. But are you busting a move when you're feeling your anxiety catch fire? If not, why not give it a try?

Did you know that some psychologists and therapists are now prescribing dance movement therapy to people suffering from anxiety? Dancing offers a form of escapism and

62

distraction from worrisome thoughts. It lets us come back deeply to our body through breath and movement, both of which are gateways to a calmer mind.

Sometimes we need to get out of our minds and into our bodies. Often we treat the body as a vehicle to the mind, which is a healthy and accurate way to look at the mind-body relationship, for sure; but we also must remember to turn off the mind and turn on the body. Understanding and then using the vast physiological tools that we were gifted with at birth is a powerfully positive and inspiringly awesome way to enhance—and maybe even enjoy—life with anxiety. Using our bodies to do something healthy and fun, like dancing, supports us to reduce anxiety to a level that's manageable and then to channel it properly, so that anxiety becomes our secret edge. Not only is doing the physiological work key to owning your anxiety, it's also your ticket to creating a healthier body.

Let's prescribe ourselves some dance therapy. Turn on some awesome music, and you're set to dance away anxiety to own your emotions and your body.

• • •

#OwnYourAnxiety tip: If you want to make dancing an even more impactful tool, then give yourself a few minutes of relaxation in addition to it. Research has proven that dancing combined with relaxation afterward reduces anxiety more than does dancing alone. Ready to move those hips with me?

Get a Mani-Pedi

'M NOT embarrassed to say that I love to get manicures and pedicures, and the salon loves me because I pass on the polish, which means less work for them. Not only are manicures and pedicures one of the most relaxing things I can treat myself to, they make my hands and feet look and feel amazing. If you've seen the extremities of some guys, you know that we often ignore them. Women tend to be better than men at taking care of their hands and feet, and many have long embraced the relaxing power of hand and foot treatments. We mustn't forget that our hands and feet need a little love, too—think about all that they do for us.

I love and appreciate the environment of a good nail salon. I love that oversized mani-pedi massage chair and taking off my shoes and socks to place my feet in warm, soapy, bubbly water. It's such a pleasure to kiss the outside world goodbye for a short while. To know that, for a brief moment in time, I am nestling into a cocoon of self-love and bliss; in this moment anxiety, for me, hardly exists.

Part of the reason why manis and pedis feel so luxurious is that our hands and feet are being touched, and these are parts we often neglect to treat gently and to pamper. So, apart from some pretty or dapper nails, at the end of a salon visit, you'll have received a healthy dose of self-care, which can do wonders to lessen anxiety.

Our hands and feet are full of nerve endings. So by gently touching and intentionally loving them, we are pleasing our body in a profound way. Our feet and hands deserve a little love, too.

And if you can't afford the nail salon right now, that's okay, too! You can create your own home treatment by soaking your hands or feet in a bucket of warm, soapy water and giving yourself the TLC you know you deserve.

• • •

#OwnYourAnxiety tip: At the salon, leave your phone out of arms' reach so that you can get lost in the experience. This is your time, so use it wisely. This is your life, so live it peacefully. This is your energy, so let yourself take control of how you want it to feel in your beautiful body.

23

Practice Self-Touch

WE TALK about self-love all the time. It's all the rage and I think it deserves to be; it's an integral part of feeling complete and being grateful for ourselves. But what we don't hear enough about is self-touch. Self-touch refers to things like massaging the body and simply treating it with respect and loving kindness.

Why do we look in the mirror and habitually find a feature that we don't like rather than focusing on a feature that we love? Why do we look at our bodies and always find something lacking?

Self-touch helps us reconnect with our bodies emotionally while at the same time calming us down physiologically. A couple of years ago at Wanderlust, which is among the world's largest wellness festivals, one of my favorite yoga instructors, Justin Haley, had us bring our knee to our mouth and give it a kiss while doing a one-legged plank. He invited us to whisper "I love you" to ourselves as we did this. Was it "out there"? Maybe. But at the same time, that moment was special, a moment in which I reconnected with my self-worth and gave gratitude. I remember feeling incredibly calm and at peace after that session. I was far from anxious.

Why not take a moment now and try one of the following self-touch techniques:

Self-massage: Use one hand to give your other hand a deep, loving hand-massage. Let the thumb do most of the work here. Feel free to bring that massage hand up your arm and, using all your fingers, massage your forearm. As you do this, breathe slowly and peacefully.

Tickle yourself (just try it!): Place one hand on any part of your body that feels natural—forearm, leg, belly, back of the neck, for example—and tickle the skin there. Focus all your thoughts on the sensation. Breathe slowly and deeply from the nose to your belly. You've just done something totally ridiculous, and it made you laugh! Mission accomplished.

Give yourself a kiss (but don't make it weird):

- *Option 1:* Hold yourself in a high plank, both palms on the floor, both feet on the ground (on the ball joints of your toes, or your knees can be on the ground for an easier option). Bring one knee toward your mouth. Once it's there, pause, and give it a big kiss. Switch legs.

- *Option 2:* Bring the back of your hand to your mouth and give it a gentle, meaningful kiss of gratitude. Continue to kiss, moving from the base of the back of your forearm upward to your elbow. Breathe slowly. Give thanks.

24

Keep Something Grounding with You

YEARS AGO, I had my eye on this particularly beautiful watch. I'd stare at it in the shop window and I desperately wanted to own it. It was a symbol of "making it" in business—the marketers clearly had me good.

I didn't wear a watch at the time. And I thought that was no problem at all. This was when I was becoming increasingly aware of my anxiety, which was growing in parallel with my business. My concentration was slipping, cyclically leading to more anxiety and shaming self-talk.

Determined to figure out the root cause of my problems, I realized one issue was my wrist. "What time is it?" I'd ask whomever was near me. I'd constantly be digging in my pockets for my cell phone to check the time and then getting way too distracted by the notifications—I was in *deep*. You may not know this, but experts of the mind design smartphones to include attributes that stimulate us and make our phones addictive. In constantly checking my phone to see the time, I became lost in the distractions and anxious about getting back to where I was before the distraction.

Many people with anxiety find
that one of their triggers is feeling lost.

Not knowing the time made me feel lost. And once I put on a watch, there it was—the feeling of now was right on my wrist. I didn't have to search out a clock or a stranger or my phone to make me feel grounded; instead, I could just look at my own wrist.

I realize this is a very personal response to the wristwatch. I feel better knowing the time, whereas some anxiety-prone people may experience higher anxiety when wearing a watch. That's the beauty of life: We're all different! The point remains the same—carry or wear something on your physical being that makes you feel grounded and connected. For me, it's a watch. Unless I'm on vacation, in which case my watch can stay in the hotel! For you, it might be a necklace or your handbag or a photo of your kids in your wallet. Whatever it is, it should make you feel centered and present . . . and it should make you feel found rather than lost.

I also want to point out that your watch doesn't have to cost a fortune to serve you well, neither does your handbag, your necklace, nor whatever else. Although I once coveted that fancy, expensive watch, I now often wear one that's significantly less expensive. Guess what? I don't feel as anxious when wearing the cheaper watch because I don't worry about it being stolen. So it's not the price tag of the item—oh no, definitely not, my friends—it's the utility of the item.

Do you know what time it is? Time to own your anxiety. (Was that lame?)

25

Laugh More Often

YOU'RE LATE. There's traffic. You can't find parking. You slept in. Whatever. You're clearly going to be late. And this is not something you're okay with. So you're feeling off. You're beating yourself up, seriously self-shaming.

What if, instead, under your breath or really loud and proud, you laugh? It'll feel weird at first. But slowly it'll start to feel amazing. You'll feel assured, like you have a little secret strategy to save the day. You'll calm down and realign with the state you want to be in. It'll feel empowering and funny at once.

Laughter therapy is real, my friends. It's been shown to help cancer patients reduce anxiety, depression, and stress. And, unlike other therapies, you can laugh anywhere and you don't need anyone's help. It's all up to you.

Imagine you're about to give a speech and you feel anxious. Just laugh. Laughing can release endorphins that counter stress. It also works against depression.

Now, put this book down and laugh for fifteen seconds. Tell me what happens. I bet you'll feel better before those fifteen seconds are up.

26

Walk

SOME OF THE greatest leaders, revolutionaries, creators, and icons of all time were walkaholics. And that's a fine compulsion to have. Aristotle would instruct his students while walking, and so they were called *Peripatetics*—travelers or wanderers. Sigmund Freud would often take emergency meetings or analyze key findings while calmly walking about. Charles Dickens would walk to clear his mind from the stressful work of writing. Beethoven would take long walks in the valleys of Vienna to get his juices flowing. American president Harry S. Truman is said to have walked a mile or two in his suit at five in the morning. And, you may have heard that Steve Jobs, who was riddled with both angels and demons (aren't we all?), would take "walking meetings."

How's that for a list of great minds who were also great walkers? So throw your kicks on and go for a walk! Doing so can change the internal dialogue in your mind. When I have an episode of anxiety and want to go from it owning me to me owning it, I walk to peacefully protest my emotions getting the best of me. We can all do that. No emotion is fully bad or fully good; there are aspects that can empower us and many that can do the opposite.

Walking is an easy and beautiful way to reconnect with the world. Just get out there, breathe the air, and focus on the beauty—even if you have to search for it. It will calm you down. When you're calmer, it's a hell of a lot harder to be anxious.

As someone who works from home a lot, I often feel cooped up. Sometimes I don't connect with anyone all day long, and that can get to me in powerful ways, sending me on an anxiety spiral right into self-doubt. When I'm conscious of this, I know that one of the best things I can do—even if I'm energetically low and don't feel like it—is go for a walk.

When I was first building Notable, times were super-hard. I was going at it alone, I was flat broke, and looking back, I really didn't have the mental skills needed to thrive while building a company in the solitary environment of my living room. I felt chained down. My body craved air, light, birds chirping, and sun. When you're inside for too long, you may find yourself thinking about things that bring you down, maybe even obsessing about them. I've even found myself manufacturing fake worries, all because I'm static and not engaging with the natural or social world.

If any of this resonates with you, if you're nodding along, saying, "Yup. I've done that," then I highly recommend getting outside. Go for a quick walk. It's as easy as dressing for the elements and choosing to move. Don't get caught up with how you look and what you're wearing. This isn't a beauty contest. This walk is for you. You're doing this for your mind, for your body, for your soul. This is self-love, baby!

If you're feeling particularly anxious, you might even go on a beauty walk, focusing your thoughts on finding the beauty and marvels around you. This is a surefire cure for negative

Get out there,
breathe the air,
and focus
on beauty—
even if you have
to search for it.

. . . .

thinking. Thoughts are a habit: A beauty walk can break negative thought spirals. Give it a try!

Here's how:

Step 1: Put on comfortable shoes.

Step 2: Mindfully begin breathing through your nose, taking full nose-to-belly breaths. (See the first tip in this book.)

Step 3: As you walk, focus on beauty. Look for beauty all around you—in the trees, the grass, the sky, the buildings, the people who pass by, the animals, the insects.

Step 4: Notice what you see, smell, and hear. What do you feel on your skin? Turn your observations into thoughts. (For example, *Those bird calls sound sweet, like music.*)

Step 5: When your beauty walk is interrupted by a negative thought, reframe it. (For example, reframe thoughts such as *Why am I doing this? I don't have time for this. No wonder I'm not getting promoted* . . . to thoughts such as *By taking care of my mind, I will be able to do better in every aspect of my life.*)

Step 6: At the end of your walk, take a moment to mentally record your beauty experience. This is your own private beauty inventory. No one can take it away from you.

Getting outside in nature is a gift. Be grateful for the opportunity to use the body you were given and the mind that lets you see yourself, and treat yourself to what your soul needs.

• • •

#OwnYourAnxiety tip: Stay off of your cell phone when you walk! As you take in the beauty, treat yourself to solitary time, no technology needed.

27

Avoid Foods
That Hurt You

GLUTEN, LACTOSE, shellfish, nuts, seeds, fruits, vegetables—these days, many people seem to have an allergy that messes them up or slows them down. There are plenty of foods out there that I call "suspect foods"—meaning foods that are likely to lead to all kinds of trouble and that indirectly or directly cause your anxiety to flare. You eat them and, next thing you know, you're desperately rushing to find and finish in the bathroom, aren't present in a meeting, or are afraid to travel where you need to go.

If you want to own your anxiety, it's crucial to know what food works with you and which work against you. But that's not enough. So many people know certain foods work against them, but they eat them anyhow. Is the taste *so good* that you can't live without it? Ask yourself: Is it really worth it?

For many years, I've been challenged by lactose. And by that I mean it made me sick. Super-sick. I spent a solid ten years fighting the reality that I was highly allergic to dairy products. I took lactose pills and hoped I'd be okay. Some-times the pills worked; other times they didn't, and I felt terrible. I'd be on the road or in the middle of a class or a meeting and—boom!—my body would have a toxic reaction. I felt that if I didn't find the restroom fast, a major accident was going to happen. If that's not anxiety-causing, I don't know what is. Still, it took me a long time to own up to the truth—me and dairy don't get along.

Sound familiar? My friends, when you eat something that you *know* is going to hurt you, you're loving the food more than yourself. That's self-destructive.

If what I've described sounds like something you've done or do, consider cutting out whatever food is causing you grief. Why let a food get in the way of you owning your anxiety? Put things in your body that will empower you and cut out what won't.

Loving food more than you love yourself is self-destructive.

· · · · · · · · · ·

28

Eat Regular Meals

FOOD IS FUEL. Our body is the vehicle. What we put in is what we get out. It's a direct correlation.

When it comes to eating, regular meals are absolutely essential. So many people find themselves getting tremendously edgy and anxious throughout the day and they can't figure out why. It's a headache. It's snapping at your spouse or coworker. It's not being able to focus. It's anxiety showing up because you're hungry and your blood sugar is off as a result.

The body craves nourishment, but if all we're giving it is sugar and coffee, we're going to spike our anxiety with our insulin. We need to listen to our bodies. When we listen and respond to our hunger by eating at regular intervals, we can quell anxiety.

Whenever I think of this tip, I recall visiting one of my mentors, Rabbi Jacobs, at his home in Jerusalem on the Sabbath. When I arrived, he was sitting in his study. He was quiet, relaxed, contemplative, and learned. He had a book in front of him and a plate of sliced green apple and raw almonds to one side. He read and then stopped, took an almond and chewed, mindfully, carefully, deep in thought. I could almost see the connection between his mind's work and the food that fueled it.

It's easy to lose track of time and forget to eat. To make it a habit, imagine that eating at least three times a day is a requirement—it's a task that you must do. You have responsibilities at work, with family, and with your life, so why not make this one nonnegotiable? Eating three meals a day is one of your responsibilities. *Always.*

If you find it challenging to do this, plan ahead. Make sure that you leave yourself, at minimum, time for breakfast in the morning, lunch in the afternoon, and dinner in the evening. By nourishing your body, you're owning your anxiety. You're committing to giving your body what it needs. Get ready to feel better, brighter, and happier.

29

Eat Wisely

B IO-INDIVIDUALITY is a really cool thing. It means that our biology is different from person to person. What works for one may hurt another. "One man's food is another man's poison," so they say. Have you ever noticed that when you eat a certain food and your friend eats the same thing, you might not feel identically afterward? That's bio-individuality at work. The good news is that we know eating balanced meals can greatly reduce our anxiety, regardless of bio-individuality.

Here are some overall tenets to keep in mind if you're interested in a balanced diet that reduces anxiety:

Choose your plate wisely: Choose what's going on your plate. You want your plate to be full of natural color—think brightly colored fruits and veggies. Have a lean protein at every meal. It can be animal-based, dairy (such as Greek yogurt or cottage cheese), or plant-based/legumes (beans). Some people can handle grains and others can't. If you can, choose a healthy whole grain. Similarly, some can handle dairy and some can't.

If you can't, try cutting it out and including another protein source. There's something out there for everyone!

Avoid processed food: Processed foods are full of preservatives and chemicals that don't fuel your body. Think fresh, whole, real.

Use moderation and consume a variety of foods: If you love getting your protein from salmon, that doesn't mean you should eat salmon seven days a week. And, similarly, if your lunch included broccoli, tomatoes, and sweet potato, then for dinner try cauliflower, asparagus, and mushrooms. You get the idea.

Observe: After each meal, check in for a moment to see how you're feeling. Are you calm and satisfied? Do you feel geared up and tense? If you're not feeling great or you're all keyed up on artificial sugars, your anxiety is probably going to spike. Give yourself a moment to evaluate the impact—good or bad—of the foods you ate. This self-check-in can lead to a calmer, more intuitive lifestyle, so I highly recommend getting in the habit.

30

Plan Your Meals

EVER BEEN that person who eats a whole bunch of garlic or onions before realizing you're going on a big date or you have a meeting in a really small boardroom? Can you see how some foods increase your anxiety levels mentally— and we're not even talking about junk foods here.

I love spice and flavor as much as the next person, but I know they can cause digestive havoc sometimes, not to mention other side effects. Some foods have been associated with doing funky things to our breath, too. You'd be amazed by how many people have told me that their anxiety spiked just because they felt self-conscious after eating garlic or lots of spice. It happens!

If you're one of those people who become anxious over such things, get in the habit of thinking about your schedule before you indulge in tasty spicy food, garlic, and onions. I'm here to help you shine a mindful light on what we call "surface-level anxiety." These are actions or events that create unnecessary anxiety on the surface and are easy to change.

So what do you do? Plan! Yes, that's it. Save the spice and seasoning for when you're in a comfortable setting with people who won't care how you smell (or who will happily indulge with you).

Go to town when you're not worried about your night on the town.

• • •

#OwnYourAnxiety tip: Surface-level anxiety is real. It refers to those things that we do or don't do that often cause anxiety. These are easily avoidable, just as with not eating food that makes you anxious. Other examples include:

- not saying or doing something that you'll regret;

- not staying up late or drinking too much alcohol if you have an early meeting;

- not wearing something that makes you feel self-conscious;

- not leaving your bathroom a mess when you're having houseguests;

- not blowing your bucks on something you can't afford.

  You get the idea, right?

31

Eat Calming Foods

OKAY, HERE we go. These are my personal tips on how to optimize the food you put in your body. Please remember bio-individuality, though. We are all different, so not everything here may apply to you. These are recommendations for foods that may calm you down, not hard-and-fast rules that you should blindly adopt. Got it?

Good Fats

High-fat and low-sugar diets have been found to reduce anxiety. Just remember that we're here on a journey to holistically own anxiety in a healthy way; therefore, don't eat just *any* high-fat food. Be smart about what you choose to take in. Healthy high-fat foods include avocados, almonds, hemp and chia seeds, fatty fish, and whole eggs.

These foods are easy to incorporate into your diet and, personally, I find them really tasty, too. Here are some easy tips for including high-fat foods in your meals and snacks:

- Add avocado to a salad, or eat it right out of the skin.
- Keep raw almonds nearby, so you always have access to a super-healthy snack.
- Add hemp or chia seeds to your smoothies or to yogurt.
- Keep hard-boiled eggs in your fridge for a protein-rich snack.

Essential Vitamins

Vitamin B: Multiple scientific research findings have uncovered that a deficiency in vitamin B may lead to increased levels of anxiety and other mental health problems. Are you getting enough? Vitamin B is made up of B_1, B_2, B_3, B_5, B_6, B_7, B_9 (also known as folate), and B_{12}. And while many foods contain some of these, it's important to get the right amount. (Note: You want just enough, not too much or too little. There have been reports that too much of certain B vitamins can cause anxiety to spike.)

This family of vitamins can have a major impact on your anxiety, so please look into this further through a specialist or physician. At minimum, consider a vitamin B supplement and know that poultry, fish, fortified cereals (my least-favorite and least-recommended source because they are typically highly processed), beans, and some vegetables and fruits offer vitamin B.

Magnesium: Magnesium deficiency can lead to various mental health problems. Magnesium regulates our nervous system, which is key to calming our nerves.

Antioxidants—vitamins A, C, and E: Antioxidant deficiency in key vitamins, such as A, C, and E, can trigger anxiety. Please make sure that you're getting the right amount of these antioxidants either naturally or through supplements.

Be smart about
what you
choose to take
in. Nourishment
is a choice.
Be empowered
by this choice.

· · · · · · · · ·

Foods That Will Help You Own Your Anxiety

Hummus: If you follow me online, you already know that I'm a serious hummus aficionado. But what you may not know is that hummus has been proven to reduce anxiety. That's because the main ingredient in hummus is chickpeas, which are high in tryptophan, the amino acid that helps our brain produce serotonin, a key neurotransmitter for owning anxiety.

Asparagus: This easy-to-cook and easy-to-eat vegetable is high in some essential B vitamins, such as B_{12} and folate, which convert to folic acid. Low levels of folic acid have been linked to anxiety and depression.

Brazil nuts: Studies have shown that a key nutrient for improving mood is selenium. Brazil nuts are a super-high source of selenium. Since people lacking this nutrient seem to be more likely to be depressed, it's a no-brainer to snack on a few of these.

Chicken and turkey: Like hummus, both chicken and turkey are high in tryptophan. So, if you want to chill out and help your brain release serotonin, consider eating more of these meats.

• • •

#OwnYourAnxiety tip: If you like vegetable juices, try adding turmeric—a powerful antioxidant and anti-inflammatory that has also been shown to have anti-anxiety effects. And drink ginger tea or add ginger to soups or stews. Ginger has been known to reduce anxiety, aid digestion, and boost the immune system.

PART 2

OWN YOUR MIND

· · · · · · · ·

MAHATMA GANDHI is widely quoted as having said, "Your beliefs become your thoughts, your thoughts become your words, your words become your actions, your actions become your habits, your habits become your values, your values become your destiny."

There's a reason why so many sages and deep thinkers emphasize the importance of the mind. Creating a life that you want starts with your mind. Within your mind, you have the life-enhancing opportunity to choose how you see the world, yourself, and your anxiety. Within your mind, you have limitless potential and abundant possibilities. Within your mind, and nobody else's, your capable voice is waiting, ready to shift the internal conversation.

Part 2 of our journey together will open your mind to sweet, new ways that you can turn up the volume on what your mind really wants and dial down the intensity of what it doesn't. In the following pages, you will learn strategies that can serve as water for the garden that is your mind. These tools are all well-researched, practiced, and effective. Are you ready to allow them to do their work? Read with focus. Be a student. The power of expanding your mind fully depends on your willingness to surrender to new possibilities.

32

Practice Mindfulness

LET'S KEEP this super-simple. Mindfulness just means awareness. It means to be more thoughtful. To heighten your
state of consciousness. If I only had one minute to help
someone with their anxiety I would talk about mindfulness.
This is where it all begins.

Mindfulness is so important when handling other people
and when dealing with our own minds. On one memorable trip
to the airport in Lake Tahoe, after I spoke at the Wanderlust
festival, my driver was a free-spirited artist who left her corporate job in New York to live in this beautiful place. We chatted
about asking others for advice. She said, "I've stopped asking
people for advice. I have enough of my own thoughts." How
true is that?

In the early stages of writing this book, I had a pretty destr-
uctive conversation in my mind. It went like this: *I've wanted
to write a book since I was sixteen years old. But how on earth
will I do it? English was my worst subject. I'm pretty stupid. I
was in and out of the learning disability class for years.*

Have you ever done that? Had self-deprecating thoughts that left you anxious and defeated? You're not alone.

Enter mindfulness.

Instead of letting the evil, negative part of my mind own the pure, beautiful part, I decided that I—the real me, who I love—would end this conversation in control. I mindfully decided that I deserve better. We all do.

With love and faith in the universe and myself I changed my thoughts: *You ran an online magazine for almost ten years. You reviewed, wrote, and read thousands of articles and hired every writer and editor who worked at the company. Forget about your so-called learning disability. The real disability is being mentally weak. This project might help some people. If it helps even one person, that's plenty. You've got this.* That's mindfulness in action. Mindfulness has evolved every aspect of my life and reduced my anxiety. And it can for you, too.

Mindfulness is to be present to our entire world: our thoughts, behavior, energy, happiness, hunger, emotions, feelings, and our anxiety. Our world includes things outside of us, such as sounds, feelings, and smells. In a mindful state, we observe our interactions with all these things. By pausing to observe, we create the space to modify our interaction with an experience so that it serves us.

Every part of life begins and ends with our thoughts. By putting yourself in a state of mindfulness 24/7, you can manage thoughts so that they don't control you.

Remember this: We never willingly want to be someone who complains a lot or is rude or jealous. But often we don't even know that we're behaving this way. Sometimes we'll "snap out of it" and see what we're thinking and how we're acting, but let's get serious, we often don't see ourselves clearly. All that can change when being mindful becomes your way of living, your way of owning anxiety.

Our thoughts can be directed to help us. When we think an anxiety-provoking thought, it causes anxious feelings or behaviors. But when we're mindful, we create a new mental pathway, and we can *change the thought*. Instead of letting the anxiety-provoking thought get the best of us, we can observe it, think about why it's happening, and then proactively do something to change it. In response to a negative thought, we can remind ourselves that bad things probably won't happen, most of the time, or that we're not such horrible people.

We can use our minds to elevate the way we live. Our breath and the food that we eat can be savored rather than inhaled. What we hear can be listened to and our words can be said with intention, not by reflex. We can treat others and ourselves with love and appreciation, intentionally. Our minds are waiting for us to maximize them. And, just like a muscle, they need to be developed or they will become weak and atrophy. By working on our minds more through mindfulness, we move from an anxiety-filled, negative feeling to a positive, optimistic, self-loving way of living.

Here's how to create an empowering and effective anxiety-to-mindfulness relationship:

Step 1: When you notice you're anxious, let that be a trigger to practice mindfulness. For example, when you notice your racing heart or sweaty palms (that's anxiety), check in, using your mind (this is mindfulness).

Step 2: Visualize a blank canvas in front of you. What will you put on your canvas? Use a tool that will take you from an anxious state to a manageable place. You might practice NTB (nose-to-belly) breathing, smiling, or gratitude.

Step 3: Once your anxiety is lessened, take a moment to identify what set it off. Now you're in a place to understand your anxiety more deeply. Here is where you grow.

33

Make Time
for Rituals

A LOT OF authorities are saying that, despite incredible tech advances, productivity isn't going up. How crazy is that? We can get to the moon faster than ever, our calendars sync automatically across all devices, our Facebook profiles seem to allow us to sign up to anything and everything by clicking one button, but we are *less* productive! Well, it's because we're bloody overwhelmed with commitments, responsibilities, and random hobbies that we often like but don't love.

How do we make time for ourselves? For our own sanity? For the things that we know are going to seriously help us make a positive change toward mastering our mental health and owning anxiety? Through the power of rituals.

Aryan, my yoga guru, doesn't do yoga without savasana (a relaxation pose) at the end of his practice.

Rabbi Jacobs, my spiritual guru, doesn't start his day without prayer.

My dad doesn't go a day without a nap or three days without a workout.

I don't start a day without ten breaths of gratitude.

What about you? Do you have a well-thought-out ritual that positively contributes to your life?

If anxiety stems from fear of the unknown, then rituals create more known.

Rituals can help you feel more grounded, stable, and certain. I suggest considering a few areas of your life and creating a positive ritual within each. Here are the musts:

Morning ritual: Every morning needs something positive and centering. Make time in your morning for you, before your responsibilities begin. The sooner upon rising that you implement a ritual, the more positive you can feel. Think of a few things that you're grateful for and either write them down or give breaths of gratitude. (See tip 67, "Give Gratitude.") You might also pray, exercise, practice yoga, meditate.

Evening ritual: Before bed is a key time to treat yourself. Learn something inspirational. Find peace within by focusing on and recapping three good things that happened during the day. Enjoy a cup of herbal tea, a calming meditation, or a quick prayer.

Food ritual: Food is fuel. It helps us so much with our anxiety and overall health. Create a ritual by incorporating one new positive food into your life and eat this food daily. Maybe it's a new fruit or vegetable that you enjoy or perhaps it's one very healthy meal daily.

34

Meditate

ET'S KEEP this really simple. Meditation is basic. All it requires is to sit in stillness and focus your thoughts on one thing. It doesn't need to be complex or complicated. Just sit, breathe deeply and slowly (do NTB, nose-to-belly, breath), and try not to let the mind wander. When it does, that's okay. Just bring it back to the breath.

I love using meditation as a way to quell my anxiety because it *seriously works*. It's crazy how I can literally witness anxiety run for the hills. When we can sit in stillness, anxiety doesn't stand a chance.

Just the other day, I could feel my heart beating out of my shirt as if there were a little chihuahua pup in there trying to kick its way out. Maybe you've felt this before, too. Perhaps when your boss pressures you at work or when a client calls you out on something and you're worried that they may take their business elsewhere. Maybe you worry that you'll lose your job if you don't nail a project. Maybe you hear and feel that chihuahua pup inside your heart right before you public speak or when you're about to break up with someone or when someone is breaking up with you.

Following the kicking, my eye usually starts twitching. Oh, the anxiety eye twitch: I do not like it. But as soon as I notice it, I begin self-cueing: "Okay, Julian. This isn't working. Time to cool down."

I walk over to a chair. I sit. I set the timer on my phone for ten minutes. I close my eyes and start to meditate. I focus my mind first on thinking of things that I'm grateful for.

After thinking of ten things I'm grateful for, I repeat a simple mantra with each inhale and exhale.

It goes like this:

Inhale: *I am relaxed.*
Exhale: *I am relaxed.*

Inhale: *I am complete.*
Exhale: *I am complete.*

Inhale: *I am grounded.*
Exhale: *I am grounded.*

In and out, through my nose to my belly. Nice and slow. The alarm sounds and it's time to go from my safe, cozy meditation cocoon back into the world. My eye twitch is gone, and that loud chihuahua puppy is quietly and peacefully resting in my rib cage. I am free.

Long before I knew that freedom existed inside of me, I met Aryan, my yoga teacher. He opened up my eyes (well, actually, he closed them because we generally close our eyes in mediation—bad joke) to the powerful world of meditation resting inside us all.

Meditation is an incredible tool because it's easy, free, and simple. What's not to love? I know that it can seem a little

When we can
sit in stillness,
anxiety
doesn't stand
a chance.

· · · · · · · · · ·

daunting at first, but you just need to give it a shot. Try it. Stick with it. With a bit of practice, you'll find that even when you don't sit for a long time, you can still find your meditative state. And it works anytime, anyplace, just by reconnecting with your breath.

Meditation can be done in so many different ways. It doesn't have to be the exact same for everyone; it's not one size fits all. We can meditate by simply closing our eyes and taking one deep breath in and slowly letting it out. We can meditate by looking at something that we see beauty in and deeply focusing on it as we slowly inhale and exhale. We can purposely smile as we recall and relive a memory that warms our heart.

Meditation is diverse, it's colorful, it's vibrant. Although it is meant to be done silently, we don't need to be surrounded by silence. It can be done sitting on the floor or in a chair or standing, in a quiet space, in the middle of the city, or moving (but if you're moving, please keep your eyes open). It can be done with your feet on bicycle pedals or sitting in a car or riding on a bus. Even while you work. The important thing is to make meditation a part of your life. That's what makes all the difference.

35

Organize Your Life

THE INTERNET is full of quotes, guides, and tips about how to organize your life. *Organization porn* (OP) is a term that popped up a few years ago to describe it. OP showcases meticulously clean, neat spaces—and it's unbelievably popular. It's "a thing." So what does this have to do with anxiety? It turns out that organization is good for your mental health. Yes, read that again. Proven fact: Organization is good for your mental health. Want to own your anxiety? Start organizing.

But let's not get anxious about it! Don't make it a huge task that becomes a stressor in and of itself. Instead, start small and see how getting organized makes you feel. That's how I began testing this in my own life, and I discovered that organization is a beautiful addition.

Maybe you can start with just one room. And if you do, try the bedroom. Organizing your bedroom can help you sleep better and have a more romantic experience in it, if you know what I mean. We know that sleep is key to owning anxiety and that sex releases the love hormone oxytocin, which is known for reducing anxiety. So when we take care of our bedroom, we take care of our anxiety.

A research report prepared by WBA Research for the National Sleep Foundation found that:

- 73 percent of respondents reported a more comfortable night's sleep on "fresh sheets with a fresh scent";

- 73 percent said that comfortable bedding and sheets created a romantic environment.

So please don't let your bedroom environment fall low on your priority list, because a nice, neat, fresh bedroom can lead to owning anxiety.

If you've got this covered, where else in your life can you add more organization—not to become obsessed, but to mindfully observe how organization affects your mood and mental state? Remember, we're starting small here.

Some things to consider organizing: bills, calendars, closets, desks, finances, fitness regimens, internet browser tabs, meals, routes to work.

What else would you add to the list?

Enjoy, and send me some pics of your freshly organized space!

36

Don't Park Illegally

FOR YEARS, I was notorious among my family for taking chances when it came to parking. Basically, I'd park my car anywhere convenient and hope not to get a ticket. Guess what? I got a lot of parking tickets. And a lot of anxiety.

If I was popping in to a store for a few minutes, I'd leave my car out front with my four-ways on. Front-door service, I thought. Seemed logical. But the issue was that the whole time I was in that store, I was stressing out big time. Yes, I was theoretically saving myself time and hassle, but at the expense of making myself way more anxious.

So was it worth it? Hell, no!

Eventually, as my dedication to dealing with anxiety grew, so did my awareness of easy changes I could make that would send anxiety packing. Parking properly is one of those changes I simply had to make. That's using mindfulness to understand anxiety in action.

Maybe it's not parking for you. Maybe there's something you habitually do that raises your anxiety levels unnecessarily when other options are available. Give it some thought. And then, make a change. It's worth it.

Some stressors you can control, so do it, because there are enough that you can't control.

You've got this.

· · ·

#OwnYourAnxiety tip: There are many other things that you may or may not be doing, your version of parking illegally. Try any of these:

- Don't give people dirty looks.
- Don't speak negatively about others behind their back.
- Don't pay your bills late.
- Don't be late returning things that you borrow.
- Don't neglect to send a thank-you card or RSVP to an invitation.
- Don't run through a yellow light when you can safely stop.
- Don't cycle on the sidewalk. (Walk your bike instead.)
- Don't leave a lousy tip when you get good service.

This may sound like a lot of "don'ts." So what? More don'ts add up to one important "do" we can give ourselves: Do own your anxiety.

37

End Anxiety-Causing Conversations

HAVE YOU ever found yourself in a conversation with someone and just wanted it to end? It could be an uninvited conversation, perhaps with an acquaintance, or it could be a random stranger who starts chirping your ear off at a restaurant, in a bar, at the gym, or in a coffee shop. You've been there, right? You're feeling good and you have a plan for your awesome time ahead, but this person doesn't see the plan in your mind. They're counting on something completely different that involves you. WTF!

This happened to me a while ago. The morning was off to a great start. I had an awesome yoga session, ate a healthy breakfast, and then met a colleague for tea. My friend left after our conversation, and I was about to take out my laptop to work when, from the table beside me, a man said, "Excuse me. I overheard your conversation about your mom having cancer. What type is it?"

Whoa. That's quite an introduction. I took a deep breath and said, "She has breast cancer."

"I'm very sorry to hear that, but did you know that lots of alternative therapies out there might help? I'd be really happy to give you some information about this . . ."

It went on from there, for quite a while.

Now let me be clear. I care about my mom *a lot*, and although this stranger seemed smart and knowledgeable, I didn't want to discuss this with him and possibly at all. But he kept talking. And talking. I could feel my resentment and anxiety building internally, but I was giving off signals that I was very interested. I nodded and threw in the odd "interesting" or "I see." Meanwhile, I was starting to sweat, and my heart was pumping in my chest. I felt totally trapped.

Physical sensations can be the gift of anxiety speaking within us, telling us that our behavior is misaligned with our feelings. To get back on the track of caring for my well-being and to send anxiety packing, I had to do something.

"Excuse me," I said, interrupting him mid-sentence. I placed a firm but steady hand on the table in front of me. "Thank you for sharing this information with me. I've listened and I appreciate your intentions. I'd like some time to think about this and to get back to my plans now." I made sure to smile as I said this but to hold my ground.

"Oh," the guy said. "I see. Yeah, I sometimes get a bit too passionate about stuff. Anyhow, I hope your mom's okay, and good luck."

"Thanks!" I said as I reached into my bag for my laptop.

I took a deep breath to center myself. And just like that, my anxiety started to shift. Now I could channel that energy into my work.

Here's the good news: When other people derail your emotional stability, you don't need to suffer from it. You can politely

Physical sensations can be the gift of anxiety speaking within us, when our behavior misaligns with our feelings.

· · · · · · · · ·

end it. It's your emotional well-being and don't let anyone else get in the way of that. Also, do not feel guilty about it. It's okay to value your well-being. In fact, it's essential.

So how do you end a conversation when you feel trapped? Here are some tips:

Kill with kindness: You might give the "unwanted talker" a sincere compliment and then move the conversation along. Or look them in the eye and say, "Thank you," directly and gently. You could even try letting them know that you're grateful for their insights and their desire to connect with you. After responding with kindness, you can take the next step—artfully dipping out of the convo.

Excuse yourself to use your phone: If using kindness is not enough, excuse yourself to do something on your phone. They don't need to know that you're about to send a text to your friend saying you've just been convo bombed by a stranger. Just use this as your excuse to bounce!

Let others help you: At networking events, some would say that it's proper etiquette to introduce the person you're speaking with to another person who joins the conversation. Use this as an out if the conversation you're in isn't working for you. "So [total stranger], have you met Jamie from that downtown tech company?" After all, if you're not going to be terribly helpful to someone, it's best that they try someone else. I always aim for politeness by saying, "It's been great chatting with you, excuse me."

Listen to nature's call: You can simply go to the restroom to make a safe getaway. You could probably use the break to re-center yourself anyhow.

Ending conversations that you don't want to be in is liberating. It also reduces anxiety. Don't be afraid to do it. One of my first mentors said to me, "Julian, always guard your time." I never forgot those words. Spend your time with those who value and deserve it.

38

End Meetings

A FORMER EMPLOYEE of mine had an amazing knack for ending meetings. She had a warm sternness that never offended but made others feel how precious time is.

Never be afraid to end a meeting that isn't helpful. So many people deal with workplace anxiety, which is aggravated when a meeting goes on too long.

Obviously, you can't and shouldn't always end a meeting. But if you're feeling trapped, excuse yourself briefly, get refreshed—go for a short walk through the halls or splash some warm water on your hands and face. Take a few nose-to-belly breaths, think about things you're grateful for, and ground yourself before returning.

If you're in charge of the meeting, speak up if it's time to conclude, and be sensitive to others who might be feeling anxious about getting back to their desks. Leadership requires mindfulness. Conclude the meeting by expressing gratitude for your team or how much was accomplished. Then let everyone get on with their day. You ready? Let's own our anxiety and empower our people to own theirs, too.

39

Put Your Phone on Silent

A GREAT WAY to own your anxiety is right at your fingertips. Literally. Put your phone on silent and put it away. It's that simple. Our smartphones are so "smart" that they've found a way to create major anxiety in our lives.

I want you to understand something really important—smartphones, social media websites, and apps are designed to over-stimulate our minds. They're created by experts who are often psychologists. Smartphones are engineered to be hard for us to put away. They're built to excite us, make our hearts beat a little faster, and in the case of many notifications, to be addictive. They're supposed to make us feel connected, but ultimately, they amp up our stress.

Phones are a great way to stay connected to other people. But we need to manage our phones. When we do that, they become a truly positive enhancement in our lives. Years ago, I had the balance all wrong. I'd keep my phone out all the time, even if I was sitting down for dinner with friends or family. I texted from the gym, from the car, and sometimes from a meeting! I was on call, 24/7. Who did I think I was? An ER doctor?

To learn what I call *cellular management*, I started to put my phone away more often. While enjoying a moment—maybe a conversation with a friend—I didn't engage with my phone. Why? Because it was going to rob me of an experience. Now I keep my phone on silent or do not disturb when I have a really important person or piece of work to focus on. I also do that when I practice yoga, go for a run, and work out. Those are moments for me; they're my safe spaces, so why would I invite anxiety in?

An interesting experiment, aired on ABC, tested three people hooked up to pulse monitors to see how cell phone notifications may cause a spike in anxiety. The monitors showed their heart rates on a screen, indicating big jumps or declines. The people being tested were told that the experiment related to anxiety. The facilitator then politely asked the subjects if they could move their cell phones just behind them. The subjects agreed.

And here's when things got really interesting. The facilitator, who was now out of sight and sound, texted each subject a few times. Each time and with each subject, there was a huge jump in their heart rates when their phones dinged. Are you surprised? I really wasn't. It made perfect sense!

For years, I checked my phone every time it pinged. My heart rate spiked every time it sounded, too. When you place your phone face up, with notifications and sound on, especially when you're doing something that you're passionate about and love, you're giving up control and allowing yourself to be taken out of the moment. The key to keeping your anxiety at bay is to put parameters on various lifestyle habits. So put your phone on silent and put it away. Start with just thirty minutes and work your way up to sixty. Increase from there based on your own calendar and needs. You might be surprised by how liberating it is to just say no to your phone and yes to you.

40

Don't Text and Drive

ARE YOU or someone you love a driver? If so, please read this carefully and share it with anyone you love who gets behind the wheel.

I drove for years, stopped for about a year, and then started again. During the period that I wasn't driving, I learned something: When I used to drive, I got anxious. Why? Not to beep my own horn, so to speak, but I'm a pretty great driver, so it wasn't because I'm bad at it. I've driven a lot. I'm talking Miami to Toronto by myself, all over Israel (where the driving can get pretty crazy), and in cities that I moved to for a time, such as Montreal, Boca Raton, Fort Lauderdale, and San Francisco. No accidents.

So, in my years of extensive driving, why did I so often get anxious while behind the wheel?

Because I was texting.

I know it's wrong, but I succumbed to the nonstop incoming text messages and emails. I'd try to quickly bang out a response between red lights, sometimes I used my knee to drive so I could look up at the road and text without looking down. I surprised myself both by how efficient I was and by how stupid it was that I was prioritizing a text over my safety and that of everyone around me on the road. Add to this that I usually had a double espresso beside me for my morning commute— no wonder my anxiety was at a super-high level every morning on my way to my office!

I've recently received a bunch of messages from my followers on Instagram (I'm @JulianBrass), sharing with me that they, too, get terribly anxious behind the wheel. For all of you, this tip will really help.

I'm inviting you to totally stop texting and driving. Just stop. If that notification sound gives you anxiety, then use my previous tip and put your phone on silent. Give that a try and see if it helps you stay calmer in the driver's seat. Remember that owning anxiety involves directing your energy away from actions that put you in a heightened, tense state. When you see what makes you feel that way, you have an awesome chance to stop it.

Resist the urge to answer someone just because you feel you have to, right there and then. Listen, I know the feeling. Sometimes not being able to stop, drop, and respond can cause some anxiety, but that's because we're letting that notification run our lives. Let the "ding" of a notification be your cue to come back to you. Just let the peeps texting you wait until you're parked at your destination, and then write back. Hey, even better: Calls can still come through your Bluetooth system. You can talk while you drive, hands-free, if that makes you feel calm and in control—imagine that! We can use our voices and connect.

Enjoy being a responsible driver and a much less anxious you on the road.

41

When You're Rushing, Don't Email or Text

OFTEN ONE thing can set off anxiety, but the severity of symptoms intensifies when multiple triggers raise the stakes. If you're rushing, you probably already feel worked up and stressed out. Add to that trying to send an email or text and you just layer on more anxiety. Resist this urge!

What if you left the phone in your purse or pocket and focused *only* on the task at hand: getting to your destination and enjoying the process. You can channel the emotional energy and #OwnYourAnxiety by directing attention to the now and visualizing what will happen upon arrival.

If you're heading to a work meeting, why not concentrate on your goals for the meeting? You could be rushing to meet a friend or a date. Why not imagine what you want to chat about, how you want to make them feel, and how you want to experience your time together? Do you see the difference? It's transforming the gift of anxious energy to enhance us and the situation.

42

Schedule Smarter

YOU'VE PROBABLY had times like this: crazy busy weeks when anxiety rises in you and takes over. Or maybe you get anxious as you rush to a meeting? You breathe faster, your pace quickens, you're in one-track-thinking mode. I remember my exact thoughts in such moments, because I've been there many times: *Forget everything. Forget everyone. I don't mean that, but I just need to get to my destination on time. So move, please move out of my way! Okay, thanks.* (I mean it in the nicest way possible, of course.)

Maybe your inner dialogue isn't exactly like mine, but you get the idea. We're in fight-or-flight mode as we rush around. I noticed this becoming a habit and decided to do something about it. Instead of panicking as usual—worrying about time and being late and what people would think of me for being late—I took a moment to reflect more deeply on what was really going on that was making me so anxious. That's when it hit me. The meetings weren't causing me stress; my schedule was driving me cray cray.

"Okay," I said. "Now you're being honest about the real problem. What's the solution?" I had no idea! But I decided to record my meetings and commitments for the next few weeks. In one column, I listed the commitments that were important, necessary, or unavoidable. In another, I listed the optional events, which I could decline, reschedule, or replace with a phone call.

I realized that at least half of my meetings weren't necessary. Part of me must have known that from the outset.

My anxiety was my own internal alarm system trying to wake me up to the truth.

Anxiety was telling me that my schedule would be more open, and I could be more present and get more solid work done if I didn't pack in so many unnecessary commitments.

There's a cascade effect when we overbook ourselves. Before my "schedule smarter" epiphany, I slept four or five hours a night and stayed awake during the day by drinking lots of caffeine and taking cold showers. I was so exhausted and anxious all the time that I was speed-walking, speed-driving, and speedily getting angry at every impediment in my way. Sometimes I was in such a rush that I put bad food in my body, basically inhaling it rather than enjoying it.

What the heck is the point? Is it worth this mild form of hysteria to get to meetings? To make it to three commitments on one Saturday night? This opens up a bigger question: What is the point of your life? If it's to maximize every moment in pursuit of wealth creation or to make massive change for a cause you believe in, and you're willing to give up your health and happiness for it, then sure, go for it. But if you don't really want this, then design your life so that it serves you beautifully.

By making simple but significant changes to your schedule you can break these bad habits. It's totally doable and will

Live with strategic intention.

· · · · · · · · · ·

probably reduce your anxiety. Hey, it's worth a try, so here are your schedule smarter guidelines:

Allow plenty of travel time. Plan for at least thirty to sixty minutes before and between meetings. This will give you a chance to enjoy getting to your destination and to fully digest everything covered during the meeting. Afterward, you'll have time to offer that extra bit of love or attention and to log potential big ideas instead of letting them just fade away.

Get comfortable saying no. Imagine you don't take a meeting or accept an invitation. What's the worst thing that will happen? Do you really think you'll remember ten years from now? Always ask yourself, "How important is this to my life?" And remember: It's okay to say no. Your time is valuable, and so is your mental health.

Put it off, mindfully. What if you put off a commitment until a day that's quieter? We often live in such an aroused state that we forget this is even possible, but it is.

Don't be a "Meeting Superhero." The only thing you'll ever get by having perfect attendance at meetings is anxiety. When you stop trying to be a valiant Meeting Superhero, you'll be able to embrace, and even enjoy, the meetings you do attend.

When you aren't overextended, you can be present in every moment. You can be excited. Life becomes sweeter when you focus on enjoying the journey to and from your commitments. The walk, the subway or bus ride, the drive—these can be pleasurable, if you consciously attempt to spot the beautiful. Observe the life all around you, whether it shows up in nature or in other human beings doing their thing. Mindfully breathe the air. It's pretty hard to be anxious when you're doing all that!

These tweaks ensure we manage our anxiety. Truth is, since executing my own guidelines, I'm still as busy as ever, but I'm busy living according to my own priorities—and high on that list is maintaining a peaceful lifestyle while simultaneously being productive.

Live with strategic intention. It's the best way to own your anxiety.

43

Keep Your Phone Away from Your Bed

IT FEELS LIKE the number of people who suffer from anxiety today is next-level. And it is, unfortunately! Why? What's happened to the world? One of the biggest differences is these so-called "anxietyphones"—whoops, I mean smartphones.

I've said it in other tips: Cell phones cause anxiety. They remove us from our own minds (most of the time) and into the wants, needs, and demands of others. We're trying hard to stay afloat and manage this world and then we're transported into another one that isn't even in front of us! We're drawn in to the likes, judgments, and interests of others, often at the expense of our own.

Sleep deprivation is another leading trigger of anxiety. When we engage with our phones in bed, right before lights out, we are doubling up. We make excuses: "I'll just go on Facebook or check my emails for ten minutes, and then I'll go to sleep." The next thing you know, that Facebook post has you all charged up, that email pisses you off, you feel jealous of your friends' pics, you're excited by the photo of that hot person, or you're bummed out that the photo you think you look hot in only got two likes. Do you see why anxiety creeps in?

Suddenly, that ten-minute check-in becomes hours because you can't sleep. Even if there's no obvious anxiety trigger, when you engage with your phone, your mind is stimulated. Not only that, the blue light from your screen messes with your circadian rhythms—the natural sleep cycle that equates light with the time to be awake and darkness with the time to sleep. In nature, blue light is found most prevalently in the morning, so when we look at this light frequency at night, we're telling our minds that it's time to get the day started. But it's not. And that's where insomnia kicks in.

Regain your power by not relying on willpower. Why not put a boundary on your phone use at bedtime? Instead of placing your cell on the nightstand, thereby relying on your willpower to not reach over for it, make it a rule never to have your phone in reach of your bed, and especially not at bedtime. Treat your bed as a sacred place for rest and renewal. Create an environment that lets you do just that.

To sleep well, you need to peacefully pursue relaxation. If you can't convince yourself to abandon your phone for your own good, then think about the other people in your life. They need you to be well-rested. You're more productive that way—not to mention a heck of a lot easier to get along with. Who isn't grumpy when they're tired? So truly disconnect before bed. Shut things down at least thirty minutes before sleep. If you don't keep your phone beside your bed, it's that much easier.

With this empowering move, you will have more time to get drowsy, read something positive, or bond with your significant other. The days of falling asleep while emailing or texting are done. Let's regain our evenings by mindfully owning them. Here's to sleeping like a baby tonight!

44

Open Your Mind

To CHANGE your relationship with anxiety, you need to switch your mindset. Where you've set your mind will dictate how you do, or do not, choose to own anxiety.

A close friend of mine suffers from severe anxiety. Johnny is a truly amazing husband, father, and friend, but unfortunately, he has let his anxiety take over many areas of his life. It may have started off innocently, but because it wasn't managed, his anxiety has become totally debilitating.

Anxiety is like that. It's a fire—one that, if owned, can be a positive force in our lives. But if it's not healthy, it can cause destruction and desolation. I hate to say this, because I really do care about Johnny, but his anxiety is spreading destructively. It prevents him from doing many basic things like taking an elevator alone or flying, and he refuses to try anxiety-owning methods, such as meditating and feeling gratitude for the many gifts in his life.

**When we think we can't do something,
we've already given up the ability to do it.**

I've attended a couple of events with Johnny as his friend and companion for moral support, bringing in my toolkit of research-backed, tried, tested, and true strategies to own anxiety. Time and time again, he has completely refused to try any of them. Instead of reading to distract his mind, watching enjoyable videos, listening to chill, calming music, or breathing intentionally, he wallows in his nervous energy, only making things worse. Severe anxiety ensues.

My friends, if we want to own anxiety, or anything else in our lives, we must own our mindsets.

Take a moment now to identify what you've set your mind to. If you need some help, reflect on the questions below.

1   How willing are you to try new things? If you won't try new things, your mindset surely can't be changed. If you are willing, read on!

2   If you're willing to take a little risk, answer the following:
A   Will you try a new food that comes from a safe, trusted place?
B   Do you do things spontaneously? Are you willing to do something spontaneous now or in the near future?
C   Will you consider traveling someplace alone?
D   Are you willing to actively listen to someone else's opinion on a topic that you know about and have a firm stance on?

If you answer no to many of these, it likely suggests that your mind is set firmly in your ways. If your ways are positively serving you, empowering you to be your best and to own your anxiety, great! If not, it's time to really think about how to reset your mindset.

By opening up our minds, we create new opportunities. If you find the courage to challenge your mindset, share it! I would love to hear all about it. Find me and the Own Your Anxiety community at OwnYourAnxiety.com.

45

Say "No" More

WHEN YOU say no to others more often, you're saying yes to yourself.

I learned this from one of my spiritual leaders, Rabbi Jacobs. Several years ago, before I felt ready to meet the right woman and have a family, I met with Rabbi Jacobs for one of our special one-on-one conversations.

"Tell me," I asked him. "What are the pros and cons of raising a family versus living as a single person?"

"It's simple," he answered. "When you say no to one thing, you're saying yes to another. So if you say yes to getting married and having a family, you're also saying no to the single life, to dating, to life without dependents. You choose!"

He followed up by saying that, contained within the root of *homicide*, is the word *decide*. When we decide anything in life, we are effectively killing other options.

Even though it might sound negative at first, this is a great decision-making tool. When you crowd your life with unwanted commitments that you haven't truly said yes to, you become more anxious. More demands, responsibilities, asks, scheduling, rushing, and "being so busy" equals more anxiety. This is especially true when you reluctantly say yes but your heart and mind really want to say no.

Saying yes = more anxiety
Saying no = less anxiety

When we say no to plans, events, or non-essential commitments, we're setting ourselves up to manage our anxiety and our lives, especially when we say no to an event or a meeting in order to say yes to yoga or meditation practice.

Owning anxiety isn't a pill you take. It is a series of decisions, all undertaken with love for yourself.

Saying no more often is one of the keys to living a more peaceful, relaxed, chilled-out lifestyle, in which you take care of you, do the things that are best for you, and consistently keep your anxiety low.

Let me be clear: Saying no also means saying no to yourself when it comes to checking social media, responding promptly to every email, replying to every text as it comes in. Saying no to all is saying yes to yourself.

The biggest challenge that people seem to have with saying no is that they feel bad about it. So, instead of prioritizing themselves, they end up prioritizing others, which in theory is a kind practice, but practically speaking, it can really get in the way of living your best life. Living your best life takes real, calculated strategy that guards your time and makes the most of it. One thing is for sure: Our time on earth is finite.

Anxiety creeps in sharply when the person you are being isn't the person you actually want to be. When we say yes to stuff we have no interest in, we show up, but not as our best selves, which isn't good for anyone. Here are a few tips to become comfortable with saying no more.

Owning anxiety is a series of decisions, all undertaken with love for yourself.

. . . .

Check in with yourself: How do you feel? Commit to doing what gives you peace. Is something you said yes to causing friction and anxiety? Respond intelligently, putting yourself first.

Take a rain check: A no isn't necessarily forever. If you like the person who's asking but the timing isn't right, you can always say no this time and yes the next.

Forget about FOMO: FOMO is fear of missing out. Drake coined that one. Many people suffer from FOMO and so say yes when they really should say no. Here's something that might help you feel better about missing out: Most things in life will happen again. There will be other fun events, great concerts, birthday parties, courses, clients to wine and dine, family trips, and many more great things, too. So don't stress it. Odds are, whatever you're turning down now will happen again in the future.

Trust in a Higher Power: If you believe in a Higher Power, it might help you to think of it as wanting you to do what's best for yourself. This involves living the life that we were put here to live, fully. Yes, part of that means contributing big things to the world, serving others, but if you don't take care of your own needs, the other things won't be sustainable.

Saying no more often is going to help you own anxiety and feel great every time you do.

• • •

#OwnYourAnxiety tip: Here are some simple things to say yes to that will help replenish your soul and keep anxiety at bay:

- giving gratitude
- going somewhere early
- reading a book
- relaxing
- working out

46

Journal

WE ALL have a stream of interior thoughts. This doesn't make us crazy: It makes us human. Often, the worst anxiety results from too many voices and opposing thoughts. A choir with too many soloists. Which should we listen to? Which way do we go? We become stagnant, and that can cause anxiety because we want to keep moving. How do we sort out what thoughts we should listen to and which are distractions?

One powerful way to separate an authentic voice from the others is by journaling. When we commit our feelings and thoughts to paper, we see what's worth listening to and what isn't. There's a power that comes from seeing our mind's movements laid out in front of us. Suddenly, the off-tune choir of inseparable voices that create major anxiety can be analyzed, distinguished, and understood. The leading voice can be heard clearly above the noise.

It was 2011 and I felt anxious beyond words. Everything was going well in my life; I was in a happy relationship; my family was fine; Notable was starting to thrive with some large-scale new partnerships, yet I felt really unhappy. It was anxiety and more. I felt depressed. Sad. Trapped. Like I wanted out, but I didn't know from what or exactly where I wanted to go.

I had just finished reading a phenomenal book by Robin Sharma, *The Monk Who Sold His Ferrari*. I highly recommend this book. Sharma writes about the importance of self-reflection and journaling. So, in this state of feeling depressed and tired and full of anxious energy, I popped into a store to pick up a small pad of paper that I could use as my journal. I found a cozy-looking outdoor café to sit in and started journaling. I didn't really know what I was doing, but I believed that the process of writing down how I felt would help me find myself again.

A power comes from seeing our mind's movements laid out in front of us.

• • • • • • • • •

I spilled everything onto the paper. These emotions that scared me and that I despised were right there. But physically putting them on paper allowed me to examine them from the outside. Once I could see the cause of my feelings, I began to consider changes that would bring relief. My anxiety dissipated and my happiness returned.

All of this happened because I stopped, journaled, and analyzed.

If you want to live with clarity, be intentional. Journaling will clarify your intentions. You know the expression "out of sight, out of mind"? Your intentions aren't "out of mind," but you may be so confused that you've lost insight, meaning lost sight of your truest self.

For any major business or life decision, I write down my options, analyze them, and mindfully decide what to do. Journaling, like praying, doesn't need to follow an exact format nor does it have to be the best writing you've ever done. The act of doing it is most important.

• • •

#OwnYourAnxiety tip: Here are some ideas for getting started:

- Buy a new notebook that makes you want to open it.

- Dedicate a certain time each day to journal in a peaceful, quiet place. It needn't be for long.

- Don't overthink. Just start writing. Write about what's on your mind, questions you have, amazing things that are happening in your life, challenges, and obstacles. For every challenge you write about, also log at least three things that you're grateful for.

47

Date Smarter

HERE'S ONE for all the single people and for anyone who cares about someone who's trying to find their special soul mate. Dating can be nerve-racking. And we anxious peeps know that when the nerves fire, anxiety gets loud. You may be familiar with driving yourself crazy with questions: "Why aren't I finding someone?" "Is it me?" "Am I being too picky?" "Should I call?" "Should I text?" "Did they have fun on our date?" "Did we have chemistry?" "Did I really say that?" "What was I thinking?"

As I write this, I'm single. I'm dating and ready to meet my future life partner. I know that she's out there somewhere, but I haven't found her yet. There are the matchmakers; there's checking "the apps"; there are the introductions and set-ups. And, let's not forget the dates. Dating can lead to so many anxiety-provoking situations. It can lead to a lot of self-questioning, which can also lead to anxiety.

But it doesn't have to be this way. Dating doesn't need to induce anxiety. It can be a moment of growth, connection—most importantly to ourselves—and hopefully with another.

And it doesn't have to be so all or nothing. I've met many people who are fantastic, but not for me. That isn't a failure. That's a bonus. If we think more positively about meeting people rather than focusing only on one end goal, much of our anxiety around dating will fade away.

Let's break this down.

Growth: The most integral part of finding a partner is understanding what is right for us, *first*. It's in this self-discovery that we begin to grow closer to our values, wants, needs, and desires. As we align to these, there's much less room for anxiety and much more clarity and internal peace in our entire being.

Connection: If we look at every date as an opportunity to find true connection with another human being—even if romantically it isn't the right human being for you—we feel better about the outcome. Embracing, respecting, and hearing others is all part of finding connection, and can come in many forms apart from "true love," so let's not get tied to just that.

Understanding: When we date, we learn as much about ourselves as we do about the other person. We learn what we deeply care about and what makes us flourish. Take the opportunity— the gift—of getting to know yourself through dating.

> **Dating mindfully lets us see what our core values are, because our core values determine who we date.**

When we're dedicated to growth, when we become believers in genuine human connection despite our differences, we feel less anxiety and more ownership of our lives. Dating smarter can solve the stressful, emotional dating dilemma that so many of us face.

48

Remove Toxicity

H OW I LIVED changed when I became conscious that certain things in my life were toxic and that I could remove them. I started to look at my life holistically, realizing that everything is connected. How I sleep is related to what I do in the morning. My morning routine sets me up for a positive, inspired day—or it sets me up to feel as though a wild chihuahua is barking its head off in my chest!

My morning leads to the foods and drinks I ingest, either enabling or disabling me to feel clean and clear. This affects how I show up for work, how I treat myself and others, how I behave among loved ones and friends, and whether I'm even in the mood to be with them. All this leads to dinner and the evening. What I eat for dinner and what I do at night, again, will affect my experience of the following morning.

If we want it to look and feel awesome, then we need to be aware of this interconnection. Once I acknowledged the negative impact of toxins on my life, I had a choice to make. I opted to eliminate them and chose a life of evolution, rather than an endless cycle of anxiety. I'm still not perfect at this, and I don't plan ever to be fully, but now if I do something toxic or put something toxic in my body, at least I'm mindful about it going in, and I do things in moderation instead of to excess.

Where is the toxicity in your life? When you let life become toxic, you unknowingly invite negative anxiety in. For example, you might see toxicity show up in your romantic relationship, your job, your habits, your family relationship, or in other areas. Be fully open to looking long and hard at the toxic stuff in your life and consider how to deal with it.

Not quite sure where to look for toxicity? Start with these prompts, writing down your responses to each question:

Food: Are you eating toxic foods?

Drink: Are you drinking anything toxic?

Relationships: Do you have toxic relationships that aren't necessary?

Career: Is your career or job toxic? If so, what part and can it be changed?

Physical activity: Is your fitness regimen overly fueled by your ego? Is this negatively affecting you? Are you inactive?

Entertainment: Are the shows, movies, music, or books you consume adding toxic ideas, feelings, and thoughts to your life?

Sex: Have you made your sex life uplifting or negative?

Habits: Do you have any toxic habits that cause you harm?

Now you have a list to work with. Once you do, address it actionably and honestly. Be bold and make the changes needed to remove toxicity from your life before it takes over. Remember: You need to guard your mind, body, and soul from toxicity. So find the sources and crowd them out.

49

Drive Less

THE LESS I drive, the less I stress.

I used to drive everywhere. I was behind the wheel at least two hours a day. Driving brought up so many extra things to think about and to deal with. Parking, gas, insurance, other drivers, pedestrians. My anxiety monster had more fuel than my car!

Then I moved to Israel. I sold my car. I walked everywhere. A forty-five-minute walk became a pleasure rather than a burden. After a couple of weeks of walking, I was more attuned to the mindfulness that walking promotes. And the exercise was great. Walking became a reverse luxury. I say "reverse" because before my time in Israel, I'd always associated driving with luxury, probably because of the high costs of car ownership. But an anxiety-fueled lifestyle is far from luxurious.

Now I'm back in my home city, Toronto, Canada. And I live without a car, which is a first for me here. There are times when I experience inconveniences. My family lives just outside the city, so it's not always easy to reach them without my own wheels. But I've been going carless for about six months, and I feel way more chilled when it comes to getting around.

I walk, take public transit, or call an Uber or taxi. I get more exercise, walk in nature more (which, itself, is huge anxiety buster), and save some cash, too. Removing this anxiety trigger from my life has been a huge benefit for me. Maybe it will be for you, too.

And remember that if you absolutely need to drive, that's fine. But before you get behind the wheel, evaluate other options. Maybe you decide on a once-a-week walk-the-kids-to-school day. Or maybe you run that errand at lunchtime so that you don't have to drive at night. Whatever you choose, be mindful. Make a choice rather than operating on an automatic reflex that has anxiety-producing consequences.

• • •

#OwnYourAnxiety tip: Look at where you can reduce the amount of driving you do. I get that not everyone can stop driving to work or taking the kids to obligations. But consider whether you can walk to the store. How about leaving the car at home when you go to a weekend brunch with your faves? There are always opportunities to leave the wheels parked at home and mindfully go where you need to go. Let's do that.

50

Avoid Pointless Altercations

IT WAS Monday morning and the week was off to an amazing start. I had just finished a nice candle-lit yoga practice. Afterward, I meditated for ten minutes, took a luxurious warm shower, mindfully ate a delicious, healthy breakfast, and I was ready to head to a café to do some work. Epic start!

Then I got a call on my cell, cutting off the jazz music that was quietly playing. It was an area code I recognized. Not really thinking about it, I answered. On the line, a recorded message from the "Revenue Agency" said I was about to be sued and that I must immediately call a number to speak with an "official member of the government." *Grrrrrr*. It was total crap. A fraudster. I hung up feeling some rage.

Two minutes later, another call came in. I thought to myself, *Since these scammers are calling me again, I'm going to put an end to it. Right now. This is going to be a good use of my time.*

"Hello," I answered, firmly.

"Is this Julian, Julian ah Brass?" The caller sounded distant, tinny.

"Yes. Why are you calling?"

"I'm calling you, Mr. ah Brass, about a recent URL you purchased. We have important information that could cost you money if you don't—"

"No," I said. "I don't do business with complete strangers and what you're telling me makes no sense. Please take me off your list and make sure that nobody from your company *ever* calls me again!"

My words had rushed out in a tirade. My breath was shallow. I could feel my heart hammering in my chest. This was important. I was taking a stand. When the caller tried to go on, I abruptly hung up.

And guess what? I felt worse. I didn't like how I'd spoken even though I truly resented the call. My blood was boiling. I was anxious and agitated. The calm I'd felt previously was gone. That mini-altercation sparked my adrenaline and my flight-or-fight response was triggered. Without consciously realizing what I was doing, I'd initiated a fight. And for what? There were no tigers at my heels, and I'd lost the feeling of peace I'd had just a few minutes earlier.

There's no upside to getting worked up over nothing. Sure, there are times when standing up for yourself or what you believe in is very important. But this wasn't one of them. The key is to distinguish between the two.

I now have a rule for myself: Do not answer calls from unknown numbers. I do this because I know such calls aggravate me, and there's no good reason to put myself through them.

What rules can you follow to prevent yourself from pointless altercations? Put them on paper to make them official. Maybe keep them posted in a place where you'll see them often so that you're reminded to veer away from anxiety-provoking encounters.

51

Live By Your Mantra

HOLD YOUR mantra close to your mind, body, and soul. It will guard you through the darkness and it will light your way. I love this own your anxiety tip because it's actionable, logical, and so very doable.

The word *mantra* is a transliteration of ancient Sanskrit. It means "instrument of thought." Sources say that the first use of mantras by Hindus in India dates back more than three thousand years. Historically, a mantra was a saying that Hindus used to connect to the Divine source. Today, a mantra might be that, or it might be a phrase that reminds you to maneuver around difficulties and stay calm as you do.

How should you choose your mantra?

Step 1: Write down words, images, and ideas that bring you an inner sense of wholeness, faith, and peace. Don't think too hard—just do it! Let your mind wander freely, and write it all down.

Step 2: From this list, ask yourself: What words stand out? Which have the most meaning to me? What words make me feel calm and centered and purposeful?

Step 3: From these words and ideas, draw inspiration for a sentence that will be your mantra. And don't worry; your mantra can change from day to day, from moment to moment, just as you do.

Mantras are simply sayings that disengage you from the commotion, panic, and stress and pull you back to your true self. They remind you that you possess the strength, connection, and insight *to be*.

Here are some examples of mantras that commonly help people connect to themselves:

I am complete.

I am grounded.

I am light.

I am love.

I am calm, confident, and strong.

Serenity now.

Release.

Let it go.

Breathe.

And, one of my own mantras: Life is what you make of it.

(At one time, this mantra meant so much to me that I had it tattooed on my arm.)

The best part of a mantra is that the more you repeat it, the more it becomes a part of you. When I'm feeling anxious, I come back to "I am grounded." When I need that extra boost of strength and confidence, I revisit "I am calm, confident, and strong." When I'm feeling down, I remind myself that "life is what you make of it."

Choose your mantras, repeat them, and allow them to act on you. You will find anxiety drifts away, replaced by a feeling of inner peace.

52

Control Your Self-Talk

HAVE YOU ever thought about how you talk to yourself? Now is the time to harness the power of self-talk.

Pro athletes do it with frequency. They have sports psychologists helping them imagine success and steer clear of thoughts of failure. And guess what? This has been shown to help them not only perform but to be their absolute best. If this works for pro athletes, why not make it work for you?

How we talk to ourselves contributes to how we feel. The more anxious thoughts we permit ourselves to have, the more anxiety we'll experience.

Recall that anxiety can be a blessing. When I say this, I'm referring to *facilitative anxiety*. This anxiety is known to shift us into "the zone." Athletes use facilitative anxiety when they get on the court, the field, or the ice. If you've seen the pros jumping up and down, pumping themselves up before a game, you've witnessed them working with their anxiety and self-talk to transform nervous energy into something productive, something that facilitates success.

You may have used facilitative anxiety without knowing it—staying late at the office with your knee shaking up and down as you crush your work while telling yourself, "I got this." Or maybe before a test or exam, you remind yourself that you studied hard and know this material inside out. It might even be on a spin bike during your training session for that race you're going to be in. Simply reminding yourself that *you can* is very powerful.

While facilitative anxiety can be harnessed for good, let's not forget that debilitating, unfacilitated anxiety can have the opposite effect. It can get in the way of us being our best. This is the awful result of negative self-talk. Now you see why self-talk is a key way to combat anxiety and turn it into a gift rather than a sentence.

Let's look at how to own and direct a self-talk conversation:

Step 1: Listen to how you talk to yourself. Become mindful of the way in which you speak to yourself and of what messages you're sending. The key in this first step is to truly listen.

Step 2: Commit to changing the conversation. If you catch yourself engaging in negative self-talk, take notice and change the conversation from negative to positive. "I can't do it" becomes "I can do it." "I won't ever be good enough" becomes "I am already good enough."

The more you practice changing the conversation with yourself, the more you'll be able to manage your mood—and regulate your anxiety.

Become your biggest fan. Your biggest cheerleader. Your eternal support system.

Nobody can take that away from you. Ever.

53

Visualize

AMID THE butterflies, the thumping heartbeat, the short breaths, and whatever else you may feel when you're having an anxiety attack, visualizations are a fantastic way to own your anxiety.

Visualization, if done wholeheartedly and with mindful intention, allows you to transport yourself to a safe place. In simpler terms, that means: If you focus your whole being on relaxing, you will calm down. It helps to visualize a pleasing, wonderful locale. What sort of place is up to you. It could be somewhere you feel happy, calm, and at peace. Or a place where you feel loved, maybe even embraced by someone with whom you feel safe. You may want to visualize yourself somewhere that inspires you. The options are endless. The key is to visualize a place and a moment where anxiety has little chance of existing.

Let's practice together! To do this, we'll engage our imaginations and our senses. Begin by answering these questions:

- Where are you?
- What are you doing?

- What do you see?
- What do you hear?
- What do you smell?
- What do you feel?
- What do you taste?

As you answer these questions, use all your creative juices to imagine that you're there, fully experiencing the moment.

Let's use an example. Imagine going to a safe, white, sandy beach to watch a beautiful fluorescent sunset against the backdrop of a never-ending turquoise sea. Now, let's tune in on the place and fully imagine the sensory details we experience there.

Sight: A baby-blue sky. Shifting shades of yellow, neon orange, blue, and pink. A glowing sun lowers slowly toward the sea. The water is turquoise and vast. The waves are calm and supple, liquid. The shore is a long, white, sandy sheet.

Sound: A consistent purr of peaceful waves. A soft repeating sound of lapping. The breeze is a comfortable whisper.

Smell: Salt and marine life, the faint scent of the sunscreen you applied hours ago.

Touch: The humid breeze tickles your exposed skin. The warm sand soothes your feet as you wiggle your toes deeper into it.

Taste: A delicious, fresh aroma of salty sea mixes with hints of tropical fruit and pineapple on your lips from the juice you drank earlier.

Did you feel for a moment as though you were at the sea? Were you anxious as you read those descriptions? Or did you feel peaceful and serene, calm and content, full of love for this world and for yourself, even for a moment?

I hope you felt all that, but know that if you didn't, or if you felt something good but then were interrupted by a bad thought, that's okay! Visualization takes practice, and the goal isn't to necessarily feel the positive effects right away but to slowly activate your imagination muscles.

Visualizing is a powerful relaxation tool, too. When I go to my sunset at the tropical beach, I feel happy, safe, and truly content. Why not meet me there, or anyplace on the path to an anxiety-owned life?

54

Read

STRESS LEADS to anxiety. Reading eases anxiety. Put that on a bumper sticker? Maybe not.

But reading is a game changer. My father is an avid reader. For as long as I can remember, he has always had a book within arm's reach. I've also told you that my father is one of the calmest people I know. It takes a lot to get him worked up. He's been through so much that would take most people out, but not him. He is centered. Content.

Another one of his secrets to a good, anxiety-free life? Reading.

From the time I was a young child, my father encouraged me to read. When I was a teenager, he would suggest books to me.

"You know the best thing to do when you're on that subway, Jules? Read a good book. Make sure you take one with you."

My dad was adamant and strategic about me learning to make my own money as a teenager, but he'd always pay for books. His dedication to reading inspired me to read, and it has had a major positive impact on my life. I've sought the

Reading will
slow down our
heart rates, ease
muscle tension,
and alter our
state of mind.

· · · · · · · · ·

solace of a good book when I needed some time to unwind or to feel inspired. When I want to learn something or to be transported, when I want to get nice and sleepy before bed, reading is always there. It's probably my deep love for reading that inspired me to write. I want to help others the way writers have helped me.

There's a term for the therapeutic benefits of reading. It's called *bibliotherapy*. Embrace it and its benefits! I find it hard to be super-anxious when I open up a great book and treat myself to a few minutes of reading. Yes, even just a few minutes. Taking in the words, the ideas, the thoughts, the lessons can be so calming and inspiring. Reading is a fast and economical way of traveling beyond your own life to encounter another world. I intentionally choose positive books because I want to live in and be transported to a good place. I want to visit as often as I can.

Mindlab International at the University of Sussex performed a study to see if reading reduces stress. And it does. Cognitive neuropsychologist Dr. David Lewis found that reading, when tested against other forms of relaxation, proved to be much better at reducing stress levels than listening to music. Furthermore, reading is

- 100 percent more effective than drinking a cup of tea (54 percent reduction of stress);

- 300 percent better than going for a walk (42 percent reduction of stress);

- and 700 percent more effective than playing video games (21 percent reduction of stress).

Reading for as little as six minutes is enough time to reduce stress levels by 68 percent. And bonus: It will also slow down our heart rates, ease muscle tension, and alter our state of mind, which really isn't a bad thing when we need some escapism in our lives.

Always have a great book handy. It can be one that you read time and time again when you want to find your safe place, or it can be a new book that makes you feel like an explorer setting off on a fresh adventure with every turn of the page.

Reading inspires us to learn and to grow, according to Keith Oatley, a cognitive psychologist at the University of Toronto. He studied the psychological effects of fiction and concluded that interacting with fiction can increase empathy. When we are in an empathetic state, we are open to growth, we are more loving, and maybe most importantly, we are easier on and freed from negative self-talk. No wonder reading is good for our mental health.

As a coach and workshop facilitator, I encourage my clients and students to start their day reading something inspirational. I suggest ten minutes first thing in the morning, and ten minutes last thing before they close their eyes. During these times of the day, our minds are like sponges, exceptionally susceptible to what we put inside of them.

So keep a good book with you, because a few minutes can change the way you think, reduce anxiety, and make a calmer you.

55

Don't Watch the News

RECOMMEND NOT watching or listening to the news, because doing so can cause a lot of anxiety. A report published by the *Psychiatry Interpersonal and Biological Processes* studied people who watched news about the 2014 Gaza war. As people increased the frequency of their news viewing, they experienced a corresponding rise in feelings of "uncontrolled fear, physiological hyperarousal, sleeping difficulties, and fearful thoughts."

What does watching the news do to *your* anxiety? Wouldn't it be better to be a bit out of the loop instead of anxious, troubled, and hyper-informed? Why is knowing about all the world's affairs (which you can't control) more important than finding peace in your world? Turn off the bad news and look around for the good. There's so much to appreciate right at our front door. Find it and spread the news!

Understanding what triggers you and bumps up your stress is essential to developing a new relationship with anxiety. Make informed choices about the kinds of things you take into your psychological sphere. When that becomes your new mode, it's empowering, it's exciting, it's an elevated way to live.

56

Save the Date

ONE THING I've noticed that makes me feel overwhelmed is knowing I have commitments but not being able to remember when. Sometimes, I even forget what they are. Have you ever had that particular feeling of dread? It's like you know that something is coming up; you know that it's fairly important; you know that you said you would attend. But you cannot remember what that event was! It's frustrating. It's defeating. It can make you feel like you can't rely on your own mind. What you should know is this: It's not your fault.

Science has proven that relying on the mind alone isn't enough to remember everything, even the important things. If one important event is very similar to another, the part of the brain responsible for remembering, known as the limbic system, has trouble recording them separately. Those of us who sometimes forget important things may find that the next step in the thought process is negative self-talk. That's not good. So how do we remember?

Save the date. That's how. Record everything you want, have, and are going to do in your calendar—everything. It doesn't need to be fancy. It can be super-basic. As long as you note the key elements, you're good to go and your anxiety will stop creeping up.

Here are tips on saving the date. For simplicity, let's use the word *event* to cover all commitments, meetings, presentations, invites, and so on:

- Record the name of the event. Call it something that will cause you to remember what it is.

- Include the event's location.

- Jot down the names of any contacts, who you're going with, and/or the organizer, host, speaker, or event planner.

- If you have a contact number, put that in your calendar when you schedule the event. That way, you don't have to fish for it later.

Sounds straightforward, right? It is. You'd be surprised how few people use their calendars to save the date and instead rely on memory. The problem with that is obvious: We're not robots! We forget things!

Saving the date is a surefire way to own your anxiety and remove any unnecessary negative vibes from your commitments. Enjoy!

57

Create Art

PABLO PICASSO is credited with saying, "Art washes from the soul the dust of everyday life."

In other words, art is therapeutic. This is fantastic news for us all. Because when anxiety strikes and makes us feel trapped, art can be our escape hatch. Art can free us. If you're artistically inclined at all, and even if you're not, give art therapy a try.

Maybe you're asking yourself, "What is art therapy?" It's any use of the creative process to help with self-exploration. And whether you're artistically inclined or not makes no difference to the effectiveness of this therapy. If you're really good, you might create a side business selling your awesome art (joke), but that's not our reason for doing art therapy, so don't stress if you're not the next Picasso. Instead, get busy creating.

Art therapy includes painting, drawing, sculpting, doing pottery and ceramics, and even beading. In fact, just the other day I accompanied my mom to her chemotherapy session. In the waiting area, I noticed a table full of beads and string and a small sign that read ART THERAPY. Cool! This could distract Mom from her nerves. And the same went for me.

My mother decided not to partake, but I sat at the table and started to string some beads together. They were colorful and varied with different words on them. It was a perfect diversion. I was feeling a little sad that Mom didn't want to join me, but I also knew it wasn't fair to project my wants and needs onto her. Who was I to judge how she dealt with the stress of her treatments?

I started to make a bracelet with an inspiring message on it, a special message just for her. But after a while, I had this yearning for her help. This time, it wasn't about suggesting what might help her feel better but about me genuinely needing her advice. I called her over, and she kindly obliged.

"I can't quite figure out the right word combination. What should the message be?"

Mom suggested, and before you know it, she was right in there with me, helping me out and getting lost in the therapeutic elements of what clearly was art therapy working its magic.

With art therapy, you're encouraged to let your mind be free. You often start with a mindful self-check-in to attune to what you're feeling. The idea is to let your feelings flow from inside you onto the piece of paper (or whatever medium you're creating in). This practice supports the mind to release and free the anxiety that you're feeling.

To learn more about art therapy or to give it a go, try searching online for options in your community. Luckily, they're pretty abundant. I can tell you that every time I've painted or created something artistic, it has made me feel calm, put me into a state of flow, and made me want to do more of it. That's a good sign.

Here's to letting your inner artist come out to paint, draw, bead, and create like no one is watching.

58

Compartmentalize Your Thoughts

WHEN MY mind wanders, it goes all over the place. It heads to the past or the future—sometimes somewhere dark and negative, sometimes somewhere light and positive, and always somewhere distracting.

When I'm supposed to focus on something, I want to stick with it. If I need to dream or visualize, it's better to plan a time for it rather than to let a daydream interrupt a moment when I need to concentrate on something else.

When we dwell on the past or the future, the present passes us by. Even more concerning, though, is that when we're caught in thoughts of the past or the future, we're not *enjoying* the present. Want to know why that's a shame?

The present is all we have.

So how can we stay "in the now"? By putting our thoughts into compartments, that's how.

Dale Carnegie, the renowned and gifted personal development coach, long ago identified the benefits of this practice. In

How to Stop Worrying and Start Living, he suggests that, very much like a ship that seals off leaky compartments, we can seal off unwanted or wandering thoughts of the past and future. He recognized that such thoughts take hold of us and ruin both our minds and bodies.

Great, you're thinking. You're supposed to seal off bad thoughts. But you still don't know how. I'm here to help. It takes practice and commitment, but we can all do this. Here's how:

Step 1: As soon as you find yourself thinking about something that isn't serving you, take a mind pause. Recognize the thought. Look at it. Imagine taking a Polaroid picture of it. This way, you can see all the details.

Step 2: Once you've stored the details, make an agreement with yourself to either put this thought into a compartment so that you can address it at a later time of your choosing (rather than on the whim of your mind), or release it altogether, right then and there, because it's not serving you.

Step 3: Reward yourself for flexing your mental muscles and for practicing compartmentalizing your thoughts. Compliment yourself. Say to yourself, *Great job! You got this.* You changed your thoughts for the better. Although it might be foreign to speak to yourself like this, positive self-talk is part of progressive self-change.

This one tip could change your entire life. It will make you a more effective communicator, aid you in your career and in your relationships—and it will definitely help you quell those inner anxious thoughts. Welcome to a new and healthier way of being.

59

Decide When
to Decide

LOVE THIS tip. Why? Because when I'm making mindful decisions, I stress so much less.

We anxious people should take this tip seriously. Research out of UC Berkeley suggests that anxious people are more apt to make bad decisions when there's uncertainty. Therefore, we'll be better off to shine some light on the uncertainty so that we see the full situation and *then* decide when to decide.

Deciding when to decide requires strategy and patience.

In the process, it will put you in full control of your life.

Making big decisions isn't easy. It requires mental resources and sound judgment. So let's treat ourselves to some peace of mind, shall we? We choose when to think about a tough decision. And the right time is when we're calm and centered and focused. In this frame of mind, when anxiety is reduced, we can more clearly process the factors.

Let's get granular. Say you want to decide whether to quit your job. Instead of allowing ongoing thoughts to interrupt your days—*Oh, that was a let-down at work... Maybe it's a sign that I should make a move... I can't stand my coworker... I've got to get outta here now*—make a date with yourself to consider all the factors with a clear head. Set an actual date and time. Yes, even put it in your calendar. And, once you do, stop thinking about it until that time. Live in the moment. The present is beautiful.

Deciding when to decide removes the anxiety surrounding decision making and helps you arrive at more informed decisions.

•   •   •

#OwnYourAnxiety tip: Try this step-by-step strategy for decision making:

Step 1: Book a meeting with yourself, literally scheduling a time to completely focus on and work through your decision.

Step 2: Be the CEO of this conversation. A CEO needs to weigh out all the possibilities. Get comfortable being the CEO of your life.

Step 3: Create a pros and cons list for the decision. Write it down!

Step 4: Strategically and maturely (hopefully not emotionally) evaluate your options. Then it's time to decide. So decide.

Step 5: Do a self-check-in. How do you feel? If you feel at peace, then that is a great sign that you're on the right track. If you feel major internal friction, this could be a sign that you need to rethink your decision.

60

Change Up
Your Thinking

MY MIND has a mind of its own. When I noticed it was thinking things that were causing me harm, this made me think again. It led me to become more mindful and to begin intentionally rewriting my internal dialogue. Here are some questions to consider:

- How many of your internal thoughts are bringing you down?
- How many are causing you to talk negatively toward yourself and others?
- How many are worry-provoking thoughts?
- What are these thoughts doing to your anxiety levels?

One of the best strategic life hacks that can lead to a better, happier, more productive life is *change-up thinking*.

Change-up thinking, like most of the tips in this book, is relatively easy and straightforward. All it takes is the commitment to doing it.

Here's how: Every time you catch yourself thinking something bad, change it up with a positive. For example, you're on a plane and there's turbulence. You're thinking, *We're going to die. We're going down.* Replace that thought with, *We're going to be fine. The pilot has this under control. I'm meant to live.*

Or the change-up thought can be completely unrelated to the negative thought. Let's use the same turbulence example. You catch your bad thought, and you think about a happy and peaceful memory, envisioning the smell, the feel, or maybe finding gratitude in being alive right then and there. You could match that with juicy nose-to-belly (NTB) breathing.

Change-up thinking can be used anytime to ease anxiety. You can also use it when you find yourself judging others—change up those thoughts to ones full of love and understanding.

If you're nervous before a presentation—*I'm going to embarrass myself; I don't know what I'm doing*—change up those thoughts: *I so have this. This message needs to be shared, and I'm the person to share it.*

In a tough yoga class? *This pose is going to kill me. I hate this.* Change up your thinking: *This is all a practice, and I don't need to be perfect. I just need to breathe.*

What if you're feeling like you messed up in a relationship—*I did it again. Will I ever learn? Why do I let myself get hurt?* Change it: *I'm learning. I'm growing. I'm improving. I won't do that again. I love myself. I can get through this.*

Depending on where you're at in your personal development journey, this might seem really useful and relevant to you—or totally whacked-out and weird! I'm okay with either. I just encourage you to give change-up thinking a try.

Here's another little challenge for you: Try my gratitude test. Every time you think a negative thought, change it up with one thing that you're grateful for. Write it down. At the end of the day, have a look back at how many things you were grateful for. Then you'll appreciate just how many negative thoughts you changed up. Also, be extra grateful to yourself for committing to the practice of self-improvement, self-love, and an anxiety-owned life.

Every time you catch yourself thinking something bad, change it up with a positive.

Turn Your Dial

TEN YEARS ago, I was backstage, ready to be called to the podium to present an award at a big gala. This was early on in my public speaking career and I was really, like *really,* anxious. The MC came backstage and saw me pacing.

"Are you okay?" he asked.

I told him the truth. "I'm feeling pretty damn anxious!" I could hear my voice quaver.

The MC put his hand on my shoulder. "Just relax and turn down your dial, brother."

Confused, dismayed, desperate, I said, "My dial? *What* dial?"

"Julian, we all have an invisible dial . . . right here." He put his hand on my upper arm and turned an invisible dial there. "When you go out there on that stage, illuminate the room by sharing what's already inside you. No big deal."

I took a deep breath.

"See? Better, right?"

And here's the weird thing. I *did* feel better. Do I believe I have a dial on my upper arm? Well, no. Do I believe I have a dial in my mind? You know it. And I do believe that his message and good intentions helped me de-stress and return to a place of calm.

The MC gave me a smile that said, "Trust the process! Trust yourself!"

I couldn't help but laugh. "Thanks, brother," I said.

A moment later, I was called to the stage. I said my piece. I owned who I am. People smiled, laughed, cheered, and told me afterward that I have a knack for speaking and inspiring.

And here's a secret: So do you!

So remember this story as a fun and simple reminder that in life, often all we need to do is "turn our dial" to shift how we're thinking and feeling.

• • •

#OwnYourAnxiety tip: Scanning your life for areas in which you might turn your own dial is a great way to own anxiety. Take a few minutes to review many aspects of your awesome world. Here's how:

Step 1: Identify a few important areas of your life, such as your relationship(s), your career, your health, your finances, your hobbies.

Step 2: Take a detailed look at each area by analyzing exactly how you're functioning within each one. For example, if you think you're eating too much and it's negatively affecting your health, causing you to feel anxious about food, focus on this. Or, if you despise your job, you may feel extremely anxious about your career.

Step 3: Ask yourself if it may be worth turning your dial on those things that are causing anxiety. Is there a way to look at the situation(s) differently so that you feel great about them, while still honoring yourself?

62

Disable Your
Phone Notifications

ONCE DATED someone who complained that she had
major concentration issues. She couldn't focus at work. She
couldn't concentrate on what she was reading. She felt like
her mind was not capable of fully focusing, so she went on a
medication to help with that.

By the time I met her, she'd been on medication for years.
She was doing well in her career and was an all-round awesome person. She didn't want to be taking pills, but she felt it
was her only option.

After just a short time of knowing her, I couldn't help but
notice that she was constantly checking her cell phone. Who
am I to point fingers? I was very much the same way. Every
time a notification popped up on her home screen, she immediately turned away from whatever she was doing and grabbed
her phone. It was like there was a constant party on her smart-
phone and she was *always* ready to accept the invitation.

I started to see how her anxiety ramped up every time
her phone beeped at her. It's often easier to see these things

in other people and much harder to see them in ourselves. I noticed that just as she was getting into the zone of concentration, she was distracted when she didn't want to be.

So how do we control this? How do we make sure that our phones aren't contributing to our anxiety by affecting our ability to concentrate? We turn off notifications! That's how!

From watching this woman struggle, I learned that I was exactly like her and that I could do something about it. When I started to turn my phone notifications off more frequently and put it facedown while engaged with something else, so much of my work-related anxiety and concentration issues (yes, I have big ones!) disappeared.

It's so easy. My home screen is clean and clear now. No more text messages, emails, WhatsApp notifications—and definitely no social media updates telling me who liked, commented, or shared my posts. And how does it feel? It's amazing. I am much more in control of my anxiety because I get to choose when to respond. And, bonus: Your cell phone battery lasts longer.

Want to try this yourself? Follow these steps:

Step 1: Choose a moment when you don't need to be accessible to anyone. That's a great time to start the process of turning notifications off.

Step 2: Let anyone who may need you know that you're offline and that you won't be checking your phone and feeds as often.

Step 3: Go into your settings and turn off your notifications.

Step 4: Even though it might be a challenge, put your ringer on silent.

Step 5: Enjoy the peace!

63

Own Your Finances

SO MUCH unnecessary anxiety results from our financial affairs. When not managed well—and I'm referring
to both our finances *and* finance-related anxiety—our
mood is adversely affected. Our rising stress shows up in our
relationships with loved ones, at our place of work, and, most
detrimental of all, in ourselves.

When I was younger, my father, who's an accountant,
instilled in me a few valuable financial lessons. While most of
my teenage friends received a weekly allowance, my dad did
something different. He gave me a monthly allowance. This
was a sum that I would have to manage myself. If I needed anything beyond the necessities of life that he obviously provided,
I had to purchase it using my allowance or with money from
a part-time job. And I do mean anything. New hockey skates,
allowance. New clothes, allowance. Any fun electronics, allowance. A meal out with friends, allowance.

If there was something that I impulsively wanted that
I couldn't afford, I did without it until I could save for it. If,
after I saved up, I still wanted it, then I bought it. I'll never

Making clear financial choices empowers you to own your finances and your anxiety.

. . . .

forget saving up for the things I wanted—a little TV for my bedroom, an amazing pair of Timberland boots, a fresh new pair of hockey skates.

Gratefully, I've been able to take these lessons about forecasting, budgeting, and planning into my personal and business life. It's been a huge competitive advantage. Thank you, Pops!

My goal with this tip is that you, too, manage your finances in a way that empowers you and lets you own your anxiety instead of it taking over. If you're feeling anxiety around your financial affairs, here are a few tips that might help:

Know your monthly spend. Get numerical and add up everything you spend in a month. I realize this is a lot of work and might even cause some anxiety, but it'll be worth the time and stress in the long run.

Analyze your spending. Once you know how much you spend every month, you'll have clarity. Clarity is awesome! Fully accept where you are at. Now, determine if there are financial changes you want to make and detail what it will take to get to your new goals.

Create a financial strategy. Do you want to save for something particular? Set up a plan to make that happen. This might involve monthly or weekly saving rituals that you schedule automatically.

If you find something needs to change in your finances, jump in the driver's seat and make it happen. Maybe that's about clearing up a debt because it causes you stress. Maybe that means getting some good advice about how to do so. If funds are really tight for you right now, maybe it's about accepting that downsizing your spending is necessary for more happiness. Or maybe it's about getting serious about saving. On the other hand, maybe it's time to work harder in order to earn more. No matter what your goal is, making a clear financial choice empowers you to own your finances while owning your anxiety.

64

Limit Social Media Use

THE ANXIETY epidemic is just getting worse. Why? In part because social media use is rising exponentially. There's a direct correlation. There's even a new anxiety disorder on the scene called Social Media Anxiety Disorder. And approximately 30 percent of the population is firing up their social media more than fifteen hours a week.

Yikes! What is this doing to us? What are we so hooked on? What are we escaping from? And think about this: It's not just what social media does to us, but it's what it doesn't let us do, too.

Social media has the potential to vastly interfere with us being the best version of ourselves. It can lead to anxiety spikes and negative self-talk that hit us hard every time we have a couple minutes to check out what's happening in our social media world. Consider a few reasons for this:

The design: Social apps have been created by people who are some of the world's most brilliant at figuring out how to addict our minds to the stimulation of notifications. Every time a comment rolls in or a like pops up, our brains get excited, dopamine is released, and we want more. We get hooked. But just like with a drug addiction, the high is fleeting and yet we quickly build a dependence on it.

The aftereffects: What happens when we don't get those likes and comments? We wonder why. We think there must be something wrong with how we look or what we said. Negative self-talk ensues, and it's an anxiety-filled shame spiral.

The envy: Then we see another more popular post, someone who has more followers, get more likes, comments, and attention. Naturally, the first feeling is either jealousy or inadequacy, as though we're not a version of ourselves that we really want to be. It gets ugly pretty quickly. Anxiety and self-shame ensue. And life just looks darker and bluer.

Here's how we can use social media in a way that aligns with our goal to own anxiety:

Step 1: Limit how much time you allow for social media and when. Decide that you'll use it during specific times and durations. When you're using it during the agreed-upon times (the deal is between you and you) you can do so shame- and stress-free. But avoid screen time for thirty minutes before bed and first thing in the morning.

Step 2: At the end of each social media session, tell yourself two key things: first that social media is just "the highlight reel" of most people's lives; second, give yourself a positive affirmation. Tell yourself something like: *I am enough. I am complete. I have everything I need. I am amazing.*

Because you *do* have everything you need and you *are* amazing, be grateful for all that you have, and celebrate that amazing person looking at you in the mirror.

PART 3

OWN YOUR SOUL

. . . .

WHEN YOU connect to your soul, you connect to your Source—the very origin of your creation and that of all creation. You may feel you have little to no relationship with your soul, you may not know how to describe it, and you may not believe that it exists—but it does. It is a gentle, powerful force that knows no judgments or hate. All it knows is acceptance and love for the human being it inhabits. In Part 3 of our journey, you will learn how to feed your sacred soul so that you can own your anxiety.

At times you may feel disconnected from your soul, but you need not worry, for you never actually are. You cannot be. The soul requires a body to inhabit, thus your soul is inside you in this exact moment. Your understanding of the soul will come through knowing your body and mind, which you've explored in the previous two parts. Now, by having an open mind to reconnect with your soul, you will feel more love, peace, and unity than you ever may have known.

You are ready. Let's embark on the next part of your journey, where you will learn how to (re)connect with your Divine soul.

65

Do Yoga

IT'S HARD to be anxious when you're on your yoga mat. Yoga is a journey. So is life.

Yoga is a key strategy to owning your anxiety because, through practicing yoga, all the other parts of our lives improve—including our thoughts and how we breathe. It's when we start to see improvements in our lives, holistically, that we learn there's just less to stress about. Suddenly, we see that we have what we need, and when we don't, we at least pursue what we want with the tools to go get it. It's amazingly crazy. It's amazingly awesome.

I found yoga, by accident, when I really needed it the most. Back in 2008, when I was starting up my company and I was beyond broke, picking up bad lifestyle habits and negative thought patterns, I stumbled upon yoga. Not for the right reasons, at first. I did yoga to get closer to a girl that I had a big crush on. She practiced Bikram yoga, a rigorous form of yoga done in a very hot room. At this point in my life, I was lifting weights on a regular, very regimented plan, so I figured this yoga thing would be a total joke. Wow, was I wrong.

Through practicing yoga, all the other parts of our lives improve.

· · · · · · · · · ·

During the class I thought I was going to pass out. Within about thirty seconds, a pool of Grey Goose sweat (from the night before) was accumulating on my yoga mat. And the teacher, let's not even get started. What were all these hippy-dippy, outlandish things that she was so confidently and lovingly saying to all the freaks in the room? Was I the only one who didn't get it?

And then there was the girl: How on earth did she move like that? She didn't even look sweaty. She looked... happy!

My thoughts were not nice at all. I hated everything and everyone. Yoga sucked. But I did what the instructor told me to, pose by pose... and then, somewhere near the end of the class, I felt my evil thought tirade fizzle out. My mind took a brief break and the gazillion negative mind traps vanished. They just stopped. They were replaced with one feeling: gratitude.

Did it last? Not for long. After sixty blissful seconds, I started to worry about work and my bank account and sweating all over the place and the girl I liked never liking me back. But the experience of one minute of bliss ended up forever changing my life. I saw something in there—in me—that I couldn't forget.

Sixty seconds of bliss and eighty-nine minutes of hell.

I began to practice yoga a few times a week for a few months at a time. I wanted to find naturally those sixty seconds of bliss again. In these intervals, I felt evolved, calmer, more self-assured. I would stop partying. These positive changes all began thanks to yoga. It was yoga that got me here and put me on a path of being a higher version of myself.

When I practiced a little, my life got a little bit better. When I began to practice yoga a lot, my entire life got a lot better. Why? Because when we practice yoga, we do something that engages our whole body and mind.

Yoga teaches us to work on our bodies with awareness. There is so much core work in yoga where we use the key muscles that literally determine how we move through life. There are countless other benefits to yoga, such as toning, stretching, and strengthening our bodies and digestive and respiratory systems. And it isn't just how you move your body but how you see and feel in your body. It's hard to abuse yourself when you start noticing how your amazing body enables you to move. In yoga, we get close to our legs, chest, back, arms, and hands.

Yoga also teaches us how to breathe. Breath is the enemy of stress. Yoga gives us a chance to use our minds, because there are no full breaks or stops. When the movement stops, we surrender as we go even deeper into our breath and into our bodies.

Each yoga practice is a journey. Ideally, when we step foot on that mat, the journey starts. The real power, though, is that the practice follows you off the mat and into the world. This is what happened to me and why yoga became such a profound way for me to own my anxiety. It turned my negative energy into a positive and powerful force that I could harness to achieve my own ends. That's why it has the capacity to lead to massive change.

Friends, it's so easy to incorporate yoga into your life. Going to the studio is the way to start. My recommendation is that you go three or four times a week. Experiment with what studio you like best. Find a teacher you vibe with. He or she will be a part of your journey.

66

Pray

THE POWER of prayer goes beyond words.

I believe in a power so much greater than us, one that patiently, peacefully waits for us to call on it. It observes without judgment. It loves us unconditionally. When we pray, we connect with it. We connect with the Divine. When we pray, we feel a oneness that nothing else in the world can provide. The power of prayer takes us from the physical world to the spiritual realm. It shields us while at the same time it lifts us up.

When we pray, anxiety vanishes. Through prayer, our worries go somewhere else for a while. Love and wholeness arrive. Our souls connect with the Divine, and we receive love and guidance while existing in a safe, silent cocoon that wraps around our entire being. The feeling is metaphysical. When we pray, our bodies don't move but our souls fly.

When I say *prayer*, I'm not assigning a particular religion or reading words from the holy, ancient texts. Whatever your religion, I embrace it and respect it.

Prayer is your chance to have a conversation with the Divine, whether you use your own words or repeat those written in a holy text. Speak directly, and listen for a response. Whisper your words, say thank you for what you have been given and ask for what you need. When I first started to pray, the words that came out of my mouth astonished me. They were so real, so raw. They were—and still are—words that I share with no other human being. They're private, personal and powerful, deep, delicious, dark and light. They're the truth.

**My wish for you is that you find
your peace in prayer.**

If you don't pray but want to start, try whispering quietly to yourself, just under your breath, "Please be with me" or "show me the way" or "send me strength" or ask for anything else that you might need. Feel that connection.

Get ready: Prayer may be an incredible addition to your life and a way for you to own your anxiety. I suggest starting every morning simply saying, "Thank you." If you feel inclined to say more, sit up, place your feet on the floor, or stand. Then share your thoughts, your thanks, and your requests.

I first give thanks for my life so far—a deep, real thank you for the days and years I've been given. Next, I say thank you for my health. After giving thanks, I ask for what I need. Often, I ask for strength to overcome an obstacle that I'm facing. I'll sometimes ask for happiness and love to abound for those closest to me. I reconnect to my purpose on this planet and vow to spread love and light to all.

When I pray, I have no anxiety. I am free. I hope you will be, too.

67

Give Gratitude

THE PRACTICE of giving gratitude is arguably the leading positive lifestyle habit that we can incorporate into our lives to feel our best. When we give gratitude, which means to think, write down, or share what we're thankful for, we activate our best selves.

We walked into the hospital together. It was an early winter morning in Canada. Dark. Frigid. Real. It was my mom's third round of chemotherapy, the day that the PICC line would be removed. This morning felt ugly. Mom was anxious. She was wondering what so many of us wonder when illness or something bad befalls us—*Why me?* I put on my game face to help her through this challenging time. Soft and caring yet strong and focused. But the truth is, I was uneasy. Deep down I was also wondering why her. It wasn't fair—none of it! How was she going to get through the day and the many hard ones to follow? And how was I? The hardest things to do are often the most important, and they always come with an equally rewarding benefit.

As we walked into the hospital I saw a man in a wheelchair who was missing his legs. I thought, *Why him?* Shortly after, I saw another man with a large tumor protruding from his cheek. *Why him?* I wondered. It started to upset me. Why did my mother and all these people have to suffer? They were being robbed of their precious time on earth, of their well-being.

I felt angry, upset, protective, defensive, and cheated. But then I saw the flaw in my thinking. By focusing on the impossible questions, those without answers, I put myself into an anxiety tailspin. I was no good to anyone in that state, least of all my mom. Eventually, I realized this and shifted my point of view. I gave myself a task—a positive one—to be the most supportive son I can be. That was the proactive choice available.

As I took a deep breath, a loving optimism returned to me. I looked at my mom and said, "You know something, the man without legs can feel gratitude for not having a tumor on his face. And the man with the tumor can be grateful he can walk and move freely. We can look at your situation and ask why, or we can be grateful that you're getting the world's best health care and that we're still here together."

I owned my anxiety in that moment and brought it back to a goal: being there for my mom. On that cold, ugly winter morning, I learned that there is always something to be grateful for—and we need to look for it.

Next time you're feeling great as a result of experiencing gratitude, give gratitude again for how wonderful you feel. If you're not feeling great, that's okay, too. Now is the perfect time to search for things to be grateful for anyway. And, once you start feeling better, give gratitude again. Make it a way of life. That's how you keep the positive cycle going and integrate it into who you are.

Here are a few steps to master the game of gratitude:

The hardest things to do are often the most important, and they always come with an equally rewarding benefit..

. . . .

Step 1: Think about three things you're grateful for. They can be anything.

Step 2: Inhale deeply through your nose to your belly so that it expands, and say to yourself, "Grateful am I for [one thing you're grateful for]."

Step 3: Slowly exhale as you continue to imagine the thing that you're grateful for.

Step 4: Do this twice more for the other two things that you identified in Step 1.

68

Cultivate Quality Relationships

A POWERFUL WAY to manage anxiety is to engage in quality relationships.

Back in 2011, I moved my company out of my apartment and into a business incubator. This meant I was no longer all by myself, working from home. And guess what? I suddenly realized there were other people out there just like me, struggling.

Across the hall from me was another young entrepreneur going through the exact same emotions, fears, and excitement that I was. His name was Sunny—a very happy name for someone trying hard to navigate stormy skies. He had just launched a unique tutoring business. After a few nights burning the midnight oil, we started to chat. Sunny has this energy that you come across only a couple of times in life, if you're lucky, the type of energy that reminds you of life's limitless possibilities. Sunny was so different from me. We were from different cities, completely different cultures, had totally different businesses, and yet we became "brothers." We helped each other through our worst bouts of stress and anxiety, and for that, I'll be forever grateful to my friend.

"What makes us happy?" Robert Waldinger, professor of psychiatry at Harvard Medical School, asked this question in the form of a study. The results concluded that quality relationships are the number-one indicator of true happiness. Waldinger's study also revealed that the quantity of relationships has no actual impact on our happiness, so let's not make our lives popularity contests. Your sense of lasting calm and contentment does not rely on your relationships with passing acquaintances and party friends. Focus on going deeper with one or two relationships, because that's where the most effective change for the better is going to happen. Work on relationships in which you feel you can be your true self, in which you won't be judged or ridiculed. Build real, solid, honest love with a few key people. This will increase your mental health and decrease your anxiety.

Having a few close friends, who we know are in our corner, who are truly there for us, helps our nervous system relax and reduces emotional pain.

I have become much closer to a few people over the past couple of years, people who I share with boldly and honestly. Those relationships have elevated my connection to others, and that connection—that deep loyalty—has helped ease my anxiety in a big way.

· · ·

#OwnYourAnxiety tip: Whichever relationship you choose to invest in, whenever possible, have person-to-person meetings rather than resorting to texts and other means of communication. Real, bold conversations feel warmer. When you hear the voice of someone who cares about you, anxiety dissipates. That's what this is all about.

69

End Negative Relationships

W E'VE LEARNED about the power of going deeper in a couple of key relationships. Now we're going to deal with the opposite—having the courage to end shitty relationships that aren't serving us and only bring us down, that lure us away from who we really want to be, that prevent us from being our clearest, happiest, most elevated, least anxious selves.

From an anxiety-management perspective, why does ending bad relationships matter? Because when *who you're pretending to be* and *who you really are* aren't the same, anxiety pops up to ruin the party.

Several years ago, before I became more serious about pursuing my spiritual growth, aside from my long-time friends, many of my relationships were focused on partying. These relationships were with type A entrepreneurs who "worked hard and played hard." When they went out, they stayed out all night, drank lots, and didn't think twice about doing drugs. They were good people, sure, but the relationships were phony.

They were based on status, indulgence, and short-term highs. Over time, I realized that these relationships were preventing me from becoming the person I knew that I was put on earth to be. I put parameters on relationships with people who led me astray. Other relationships I straight-up ended. This was key to my personal evolution. Now, when I run into friends from my old days, we say hi and I'm happy to see them, but our lifestyles don't mesh. I'm closer to being the version of myself that I want to be.

I salvaged a few relationships from my party days, with people who I really care about, but instead of joining them on their party path at night, I ask them to join mine by having breakfast or lunch together.

Maybe right now you're thinking, "What about bad relationships that I can't end, and not because I lack the courage?" That's a great question. We all have people in our lives who are chosen not by us but for us and who we must relate with. Most often, these are family members, and it might not be possible, reasonable, or ethical to cut them from our lives. The trick is to put parameters on those relationships. Choose when you see them, and let it be at a time and for a duration that's tolerable. When you call or visit them, you might want to plan an end time. For in-person visits, have an "out" ready. Schedule something that gives you a reason to leave. But remember this: It's possible that the people who challenge us are in our lives for a reason. Maybe they are part of our path of personal growth, true compassion, and understanding. Maybe they can teach us what it means to give unwavering love.

When you let go of the negative people in your life (the ones you can let go), you'll find yourself getting closer to "your people." This isn't some faraway dream but a reality within reach. It's called growth and that's a good thing. We *want* that. Little improvements get us closer to a life of harnessing our anxiety.

70

Know Your Direction

IT'S VERY difficult to be anxious when we know our direction in life. Since most cases of anxiety originate from fear of the unknown, when we can see where we're going, there tends to be much less anxiety. People who know exactly where they're going, even if they feel nervous about something in life, will not let the anxiety slow them down. This is crucial to owning anxiety. Identifying our direction empowers us to thrive with nerves, not hide from them.

Let's put it this way:

When a navigator knows the way to the destination, the unexpected is part of the journey. But when the navigator doesn't know the route, the unexpected *is* the journey.

I've certainly been the most anxious, stressed, and sometimes temporarily depressed when I haven't known where I'm heading. Being directionless can create feelings of extreme uncertainty about your purpose, your reason for being, and what to have for breakfast! Have you noticed that it's a spiral effect?

If you've ever felt directionless, tell me, have you seen how quickly things can spiral out of control? Our decision-making ability goes out the window. Suddenly, the worry of a tiny choice, like what to eat for lunch or what route to take home, holds major weight and big problems seem unsolvable.

When I was creating the company Notable, I knew that my direction was to build the brand and that I would get there one day. This one certainty helped me focus on the big picture and motivated me every day.

Sounds good, right? But how do you find direction? Try these three steps:

Step 1: Ask yourself: Where do I want to be in five years? In ten years? In twenty years? Write down your answers. Use your answers to visualize the key things that you want to accomplish. What does it look like when you achieve them?

Step 2: Pretend that your final destination, where you'd like your direction to take you, consists of only three things. What are those things? Please list them.

Step 3: After completing Steps 1 and 2, write down five action points that will move you toward achieving the items listed.

You got this. Get busy!

71

Breathe before Meetings

HAVE YOU ever sat down to a meeting and felt so nervous that it's like the only person in the room is your old friend anxiety? You know, heart pounding through your shirt, sweat dripping, the dizziness, the shortness of breath. You're not alone. So many of us are right there with you.

It's rough. Meetings can be unforgiving. They can be so stressful that they can cause feelings of major anxiety, panic, and a general sense of "get me out of here"—that feeling like you're going to have a heart attack right there in front of your colleagues. But don't worry: There's a natural way to come back to calm simply by taking a moment to breathe.

Enter Aryan, my yoga guru. Aryan would go to great lengths to teach his students how to breathe. He taught me how sacred our breath is and how we must not take it for granted.

Under his guidance, I learned how to breathe. It sounds crazy, because breathing is something we do naturally, but what I mean is that I learned how to use breath as a tool to quell my anxiety, especially in meetings.

I began sharing this technique with some of my employees at my former company, and they began to enjoy the practice. One day, before I started a meeting, I asked, "Would you mind if we paused for a moment to breathe?" My heart was racing and I needed that time.

"Sure," my colleague said. "I get it." She compassionately and curiously joined me, and we breathed at our own pace, in our own "space" for a minute or so.

This is all I needed.

"Better?" she asked when we were both done.

"Much," I said. "Let's do this."

And after escorting our negative, nervous, debilitative, anxiety-evoking energy to the door, I could channel that freed-up energy into productive conversation. We were ready to start the meeting.

Taking a few moments to breathe before a meeting will not only set you up to own your anxiety but also to own your meeting.

• • •

#OwnYourAnxiety tip: Delivering your best at a meeting you care about is one secret to leveling up to where you want to be. In addition to breathing before meetings, I also suggest visualizing in advance the result you want for the meeting; using positive and strengthening affirmations that make you feel confident; arriving fifteen minutes early; and giving gratitude before it's "go-time."

72

Get to Know Your Crossing Guard

F OR YEARS, I had the good fortune of having a crossing guard one block from my home. He was there every morning and afternoon. He was there on the horrid, cold winter mornings. He was there on the sunny, bright summer afternoons. An elderly man, he wore his uniform proudly as he lifted that stop sign and blew his whistle to help everyone cross safely, greeting people warmly.

"Nice day today," he'd say.

Right. I'd failed to notice.

"You're right! It's a great day today," I'd answer.

When he guided me across the street, I slowed my pace. He went first to stop traffic. Then I'd cross to the middle of the intersection, keeping pace with him.

"Thank you so much!" I'd call out, once I'd made it safely across.

"You're most welcome, son," he'd say.

Despite what was going on in my life or how I felt about the stressors of putting on my CEO hat, when I saw this man, I felt inner peace. I felt appreciation for the amazing people in this world, that life is a circular journey.

Part of owning anxiety is being mindful of opportunities on our path to calm. Let's try our best to find others who show the way, and let's cross the road with them.

Be mindful of opportunities on the path to calm.

. . . .

73

Listen to What You Listen To

OR YEARS, I listened to hard-core hip-hop or beat-pumping electronic dance music (EDM) first thing in the morning and in my car on my commute. During the day, on my headphones I had the same music playing. Evening drive home, the same pounding, wind-up music making me feel stuck in the *brutal* traffic and compelling my mind and body: *Go! Go! Go!*

This was the most anxious chapter of my life. Was my choice of music coincidental? Probably not. Was it compounding my anxiety? Probably.

As I evolved as a person, I realized the lyrics in hip-hop were triggering me, inciting my fight-or-flight impulses. This was so beneath where I was aiming to go. The unrelenting beat in the EDM was also so intense that it induced my anxiety.

Now I mindfully choose my music based on the mood or state of mind I want to be in. For example, first thing in the morning, I listen to smooth, light jazz or upbeat happy music by roots or reggae artists such as Xavier Rudd, Trevor Hall, Nahko, and Rising Appalachia. If I want a Zen, inspired start to my day, I put on more traditional Indian musical artists, such as Krishna Das, Jai Uttal, and Jai-jagdeesh. And if I want to feel connected to my heritage, I play quiet, melodic Hebrew tunes.

I find calm and serenity from these genres and artists. My breathing slows down almost immediately. In fact, it almost feels like life's pause button is pushed for a few minutes.

The research on the effects of music reaffirms its calming effects. Let me share a few known benefits with you. Listening to calming music

- for one hour each day is said to reduce depression;

- can be as effective as massage at reducing anxiety;

- might even have an impact on plants. (A study conducted by Dorothy Retallack in 1973 showed that plants leaned toward classical and jazz and moved their leaves away from rock music.)

When you're ready to own your anxiety, mindfully choose your music. It might not be as exciting as Tiësto, Tupac, or Lil Wayne, but calm tunes are going to center you—and that matters most.

Want to take it to a whole higher level? Try putting on soothing music as you meditate, read, practice yoga, eat slowly, exercise, take a warm bath, or do any of the other tips in this book!

Now, on to the flipside: If you want to intentionally spike your anxiety so that you can then channel it into a particular area of focus, like coming up with a creative project, or really giving it that extra 10 percent at the gym, you might want to put on some of the hard-core hip-hop or pulse-jumping EDM. Just be aware that it may boost your anxiety symptoms, so if you feel too revved up, press play on something calm to get you back to center.

74

Be in Nature

NATURE IS ONE of the greatest gifts we've been given. The green flowing grass, forest, and trees; the blue sky; the crisp, cool wind; the warm sun; the blankets of powdery white snow. They're all a privilege to behold, and I feel deeply grateful for these natural wonders. This isn't the first time in this book that I've extolled the virtues of nature. Remember how restorative and anxiety-busting walks can be (tip 26)? The same applies to all aspects of the natural world. The wonders are out there; they're waiting for us, so let's go find them.

Getting a dose of nature has long been a ritual of mine. As a kid, playing in the park was a hobby. And as I've grown older, not that much has changed. Whenever I can, I sit outside to get fresh air and catch some sun. You can find me bundling up in layers in the wintertime so that I can enjoy the outdoors, even when the temperature suggests it would be easier to stay in. Living by the sea was incredible for me, and I took advantage of every available moment to hang out at the beach and swim.

Wherever you may be, even if it's in the concrete urban jungle, there's usually a park that isn't too far away, or at least a tree. It's worth finding green spaces to wander through. When we're in nature, anxiety diminishes. I've found that even when I'm crazy-busy with work, doing a deal or meeting a deadline, it's those few minutes spent outside that help me regain a composed, strategic, positive, and thoughtful perspective. In other words, nature makes me better. I'd even say that nature heals. And I'm not alone in that belief.

For millennia, our ancestors found solace in time spent outdoors and now science is proving that it is measurably valuable to our mental health. Researchers have found that people who spend a minimum of thirty minutes in parks each week tend to have lower blood pressure and better mental health than those who don't. Simply being in green space might reduce levels of stress and decrease symptoms of depression and anxiety. Being closer to nature has a restorative effect that we ought to take seriously.

Inhale nature and exhale anxiety.

75

Wake Up with Intention

WAKING UP with intention means being aware of your thoughts and path from the moment your eyes open in the morning. How we treat ourselves when we wake up— mentally, physically, spiritually—impacts the course of the day.

I have a habit. It involves looking up the second I hear my alarm go off and saying out loud, "Thank you." Who or what you direct your thank you to is your decision. You can use any name or term that you feel comfortable with. Maybe it's the Holy One, the Divine, the Lord, the Creator. It's not about the name but about honoring your own spiritual beliefs, as you understand the gift of being given another day and the importance of giving gratitude for it. And if you're not a believer, just say thank you to whatever forces have allowed you to be there, alive, ready to enjoy this brand new day.

There's an ancient belief that when we sleep our soul returns to the Divine, so when we receive it back upon awakening, it's a blessing and a gift.

A new day is a new life.

Let's not forget that the morning is when the mind is at its most vulnerable state. How we speak to it, how we treat it first thing will dictate how the day goes. If the mind isn't strong, sharp, and full of love from your first waking moment, anxiety has a chance to seep in. Gratitude can put a lid on anxiety before it acts upon your entire system. So can having an intentional path and plan for the day. And for your awesome life.

Before you go to bed, know what your intention is for the next morning. Then start by giving thanks every single morning when you wake up, before you look at your phone, before you get out of bed. This is how you can seize the day. And you deserve that.

· · ·

#OwnYourAnxiety tip: Practice channeling the energy of anxiety into three simple morning rituals:

1 Set your intention for the day.

2 Control what you let in to your morning (stay off social media, for example).

3 Ask yourself, "How will I make today even better than yesterday?" And then answer your question.

76

Define Your Values

THE MOST anxious and depressed times in my life have been when I was living aimlessly and ignoring my own values.

I'll be totally honest with you. Several years ago, I moved to Montreal from Toronto. This was totally strategic: To properly expand to Montreal, I needed to move there. Business was by far my top priority back then. I was in my mid-twenties and still had a lot of growing to do. My values were far from defined. Why? Because I had never taken the time to think about and define them. It's not that I didn't have values; in my heart I was a good person who meant well, but I wasn't aware of my role in the world or how my actions could have a significant impact—be it good or bad—on others. And I did something that, to this day, I still truly regret.

I was dating a wonderful girl. We had grown close. But one day, I realized that to make my business bigger, I had to be back in Toronto. It shames me to say this, but without warning, I packed up my belongings and left. I didn't call Stephanie until *after* I was already gone. Why? Because I was too scared to confront her, too scared to tell the truth about my feelings. Looking back, it was a pathetic and callous move. It was created by and executed by my anxiety. It does not fill me with pride.

But I have to own my behavior so I can continue to grow. We all have to. And we all have regrets. I now know that one of my true values is to be kind and considerate of others. When I go against this value, others suffer and so do I. Today, I know that my values include being my best, creating, sharing, helping others, and treating them with respect. But . . .

> **We can't be our best until we define what**
> **our best is. And we can't define what our best**
> **is until we know what our values are.**

When I feel that I'm not living up to my own values, my anxiety revvs up. It comes strong, fast, and furious. Looking back, I realize that when I bolted from Montreal, it was because the only powerful value that I had at that time was to build a successful company. I felt internal friction because who I was being in that moment and who I thought I was supposed to be weren't aligned. This is why we need to do the deep work to define our values; when we involve others in our lives, we must know with precision what it is that we really want. This goes for romantic relationships, business and career collaborations, having children, owning and caring for a pet, and so much more.

You'll create a purposeful, clear life when you define what your important values are—and then act on them. Once you do, anxiety disappears. That's big. That's really big.

To define your values, break your life into key pillars. Consider these areas:

Family: Who matters to me and why? Who am I grateful for and why? Do I show gratitude to those I'm thankful for, and if

You'll find that purposeful, clear life when you define what your important values are—and then act on them.

· · · · · · · · · ·

not, can I in the future? What are my values around family, and how can I uphold them?

Health: How is my health? Am I healthy? What do I consider to be healthy? Am I physically healthy? Mentally healthy? Both? Neither?

Relationships and friendships: Am I close with my partner? My family? Are my "close friends" truly dear to me? Am I being fulfilled by my relationships? Am I giving back to them? Are they the types of relationships that I want to have?

Career: Does my job add to my happiness or take away from it? Does it make me anxious? Am I using my skills to the fullest? Is it providing me the income that I need?

Spirituality: Am I doing the work to connect to something bigger than myself and to feel a true sense of spirituality? Am I lost or do I feel connected?

Community: Does my community feel supported by me? Do I feel connected to it? What can I do to increase this feeling of connection?

What I'm really asking you here is *what matters to you*, and *how will you live in alignment with what matters to you*? Once you clearly define your values, you can act on them. And acting on them, rather than against them, puts you in a position to channel your anxiety for good.

Let your own values anchor you, keeping you grounded and calm.

77

Remember Your
Six-Year-Old Self

HAVE YOU noticed how much more it takes for us adults
to get excited, passionate, and jazzed up about life? I'm
referring to both the amazing, big things and the ordi-
nary, little things. I mean, you're reading and breathing right
now—two huge blessings. Think back to when you were a kid.
Do you remember when you learned to read? Wasn't that one
of the coolest things ever? When we were children, it was easier to feel proud of ourselves, wasn't it? The world was exciting.
It was new. We appreciated it. We lived in a state of gratitude
without even trying.

Right now, you are breathing and reading and learning and
growing! That's massive. That's amazing. Think about the mir-
acles needed for this to happen. If your six-year-old self could
appreciate how magical life is, why can't you?

I often lead a guided meditation in which I have partici-
pants imagine themselves at age six. Then they take it a step
further and imagine the most beautiful, majestic, angelic set

of angel wings on their six-year-old backs. Want to know what happens then? If you do, try it yourself!

Let me walk you through my guided mediation. Remember: Use your imagination:

Step 1: Take a deep nose-to-belly (NTB) breath, and inside your soul, picture yourself at age six. Imagine your bright, beautiful smile. Picture your hair. What color is it? See your wide-open eyes.

Step 2: In your imagination, place the most beautiful pair of sparkling angel wings onto the back of your six-year-old self. Once they're fastened, flap them a couple of times.

Step 3: Take a big inhale through the nose and imagine your young, angelic self preparing to fly. You're about to take off; you're spreading your wings, testing them.

Step 4: On the exhale, fly out of your body into the world. Feel the wind and fresh air against your face. Feel the exhilaration surround you as you fly high above this physical world and look down at all the beautiful life below. Take as many breaths here as feels right for you.

Step 5: On your next exhale, let yourself softly land. Feel your feet on the ground. Spread your arms out wide and imagine the two people you love most in this world appearing beside you. Offer a hand to each of them. Feel their warmth.

Step 6: Now inhale as a circle begins to form around you, full of the people who have positively touched your life. Let them join your circle and link hands. As the circle grows and nears completion, allow perfect strangers of all kinds— different races, religions, ages, genders—to join your circle.

Look around at all the other angels in your life. Smile at them. Welcome them. Know that love surrounds you.

Step 7: On your next inhale, gently release hands with your circle of angels. Lightly flap your wings. Fly up high toward the sky, and when you reach the end of your inhale, fly back into yourself.

Step 8: As you exhale, let the child and angel in you fall back into your memory, where it will always be with you.

The angel that is your younger self is just a breath away. Your circle of angelic loved ones are right there when you need them.

78

Spend Time
near Water

HUMAN BEINGS have always felt a connection to the ocean. It's good for our mental health! Some studies have shown that living within sight of the ocean lowers psychological stress. Although we can't all just pack up and move, we can try to increase our visits to bodies of water. We can choose our vacation locales carefully. It may even be worth it to splurge on that ocean-view room, knowing that it's good for you.

You can also easily up your water vibe with your home decorating. I know lots of people who have hung up gorgeous pictures of the ocean, lakes, or rivers. Images of the blue water, the limitless horizon, the vast sky that appears as a mirror of the water beneath are all you need to time travel to the water.

Why not hang a picture of a body of water on your wall? Do it with intention and pride, knowing that by mindfully deciding what you let into your environment, you are also choosing your mental health. Let's go for a design that flows with a purpose that owns our anxiety.

79

Light Candles

IGNITE ONE flame and it brings another to life. The first goes out, but its purpose was to give the second life. The purpose of the second is to softly light up my life. A dancing flame enhances any space.

. For years, candles have played an important role in my life. They deeply and ceremoniously fill my home, adding a sense of celebration and tranquility. I light them when I write, when I read, when I eat. I light them all around me when I practice yoga. I have a travel candle that I picked up in Tel Aviv. I bring it with me wherever I go. I recommend buying at least two candles for your home. Pro tip: Different scents have different benefits, so make sure to read up on which scented candles to light up at home.

And, one more thing for the guys reading this: Most candles are bought by women. It's time to change that. Candles are hypnotic. Peaceful. Life-affirming.

By focusing on the candle's flame, my mind goes from focusing on my problems to feeling the eternity in those colors and in the warmth. For hundreds of years, candles have been used not only as a light source in the literal way, but more importantly, in the spiritual way. I sat down with Rabbi Jacobs to learn more about the power of light. He shared that light creates space for others. Light allows us to truly *see* others. Light doesn't just offer us an opportunity to see what's in front of us, it lets us see the entire picture.

In Judaism, the flame of a candle represents the soul. The wick is the body. And without a wick, we have no visible flame. The soul needs a body to inhabit. Otherwise it is aimless, floating.

These are powerful metaphors, and perhaps they explain a little about why we experience candlelight as magical or spiritual. My friend and yoga guru, Aryan, shared with me the word *trataka*, which means to look or to gaze. It plays a major role in meditation. Candles are used to help the mind with trataka. The ancient yogis used fire as a focus point because it is the purest element. This helped them still their thoughts.

"Stilling the thoughts," Aryan said, "thins out the blanket that we have in front of our mind. All of a sudden, our thoughts start to even out and the third eye can open."

A dancing flame enhances any space.

• • • • • • • • •

Insight. Chakra. The third eye. The sixth sense, which is deeper understanding. Wisdom, higher thinking, things beyond information, things that offer clarity and broaden perspective—all this is accessible to us through the lighting of a small flame.

Let's put this into practice:

Step 1: To meditate using a flame, place a candle in front of you, about an arm's length away. The flame needs to be still, not flickering. It is better to have the room a bit dark so that the candle is bright.

Step 2: Focus on the flame without blinking your eyes. Your five senses will feel free. Your mind will become still. As Aryan says, "Each sense is a horse. We therefore have five horses. Each horse is now free to go wherever it wants, but we're not going anywhere because our horses are tied to us, the chariot."

Step 3: Keep your eyes open until you must close them. Don't wipe tears; try not to move.

Step 4: When you have reached your maximum, continue focusing on the candle with your eyes closed. When the flame disappears from your closed eyes, your session is complete. Open your eyes again. Breathe deeply and appreciate your meditation.

Do this practice up to three times a day. As the flame in your eyes disappears, so, too, will your anxiety. Here's to lighting up our worlds.

80

Practice Self-Love

Y OU'VE HEARD it before: To love others—and to love life—
first you need to wholly love yourself. I believe in this at my
core. I believe it so much that it is, for me, sacred.

I've learned this, though: Self-love doesn't just happen. It
takes work. Yes, you read that right. Loving yourself takes
work. I don't always love everything about myself. In fact,
there are times when I'm really not very impressed with things
I've done or am doing. But, like a parent who loves his child
unconditionally, even when I disappoint myself, I don't give
up on love and compassion.

In an effort to be transparent and vulnerable—and so you
can see you're not alone—let me share with you just a few
shame-inducing things I've done in the past:

- partied too much on a night out and acted like an idiot;
- slept with someone randomly without thinking through
  the consequences;
- acted like a jerk to my parents;

Self-love doesn't just happen, it takes work.

. . . .

- ate a bunch of crap food and made myself sick (and then did it again a week later);
- called it in at work when my team deserved more from me.

What I've learned is that when I mess up, the best thing to do is recognize it, deal with any fallout (including apologizing and making up for my mistakes), and as quickly as possible forgive myself. Being consistently self-compassionate gives me the grounding I need to make real and lasting changes, rather than being mired in my own feelings of disgust and self-pity. My anxiety and shame is always significantly lessened when I can turn quickly back to loving myself.

Many years ago, in my Notable days, I was on the set of the reality TV show *Dragons' Den*, where I interviewed W. Brett Wilson, who has since become a mentor. He told me that first, before anyone or anything else, he takes care of himself—before his family, his businesses, his investments, his commitments to charities. He takes care of Brett because it's only when he's at his best that he can be the best family member, business owner, investor, and leader to those around him.

Self-love decreases anxiety and depression and increases optimism. Take it very seriously and implement it in your life right away because *it will* help you own your anxiety and be a happier, better version of you.

Here are a few daily self-love ideas:

- Treat yourself to your favorite breakfast (but practice moderation if your fave breakie is double chocolate waffles with caramel syrup and hot chocolate).
- Take a personal day for yourself.
- Get a massage or take a spa day.
- Attend a yoga retreat.
- Remind yourself of your five best qualities.
- Stay in a hotel, even if it's in the same city where you live.
- Book a trip.
- Read a book for pleasure.
- Mindfully eat your meal while giving gratitude for all of it.
- Masturbate.

By loving yourself more, you'll be able to love others more, too. And it's hard to be anxious when you're being loving and compassionate to yourself and being loved by others, too. Enjoy every loving minute.

81

Do the Mirror Trick

WAS ON a small plane and beside me was a well-dressed, very stylish woman with an aura of strength and confidence— or so it appeared. Before we took off, she pulled out her phone and switched it to selfie camera mode. I expected her to take a few pictures to send to friends, but she didn't. Instead, she looked at her image in the phone and spoke to herself and made confident nods and facial gestures. It's as if she said to herself, "You got this." She was staring deeply into her own receptive eyes. I could see her accept herself a few more times—*you got this*—and then, with ease and assurance, she put her phone back into her purse.

It was beautiful. So confident. Inspiring. Anxiety-owning. It seemed that she was approving of herself and accepting fully all that she was and all that she may not be.

I didn't say anything to her since this seemed to be a private moment. But what I felt was truly inspired—by her commitment to be her best self and to own her mind.

This started me thinking more about the act of self-talk and how doing something active like looking right at yourself in a mirror while speaking is a brilliant thing to do. And don't stress about being judged by someone who sees you. Who knows? Maybe they'll even get it—as I did on that plane—and respect you for being your own best friend.

A few rules to live by that will help you own your anxiety and improve your life:

- Whenever you pass a mirror, make a habit of looking at yourself and giving yourself a compliment—either out loud or just in your thoughts. No more negative mirror talk! You're beautiful, and you deserve to hear it.

- Don't restrict yourself to physical compliments. Remind yourself of your best internal qualities or give yourself messages that make you feel calm, cool, and collected.

- Breathe deeply, calmly, wholly every time you pass a mirror instead of holding your breath and going straight for the killer judgments and digs. Inhale and exhale. Repeat your affirmations. Take the time to see yourself in a kind light.

It's time to see mirrors for what they are—reflections of our best selves. So often we become self-critical in front of our reflections, dissecting ourselves as though we were science specimens. But you are not a lab experiment. You are a wonderful, unique, holy, straight-up-awesome being! True confidence will come from breaking the judgment habit and practicing healthier ones instead.

It's easy to practice the mirror trick. Take a good, long look at your best self. You look great!

82

Know You're Not Saving the World

NEEDED TO chill. I needed to relax. I needed to stop and check myself. I was taking my work so seriously that I was skipping over many other important things in my life. You know, like my relationships, like making the effort to put the right fuel into my body, like pausing to be grateful.

I was running a company that I really wanted to grow. I thought that was more important than anything else. But I was a disaster. By hyper-focusing on this one goal, I neglected so many things that I'm so fortunate to have—awesome friends, family, my health. I sacrificed my mental health for my work. Sound familiar?

We need to guard our mental health.
Our lives depend on it.

I got lucky, really lucky. There I was, running around, anxious, stressing, feeling constantly overwhelmed... and then in walked one of my best friends, Dave. Dave is the CEO of a giant advertising agency. He took one look at me and said, "You're messed up. I can see it. Look at yourself."

I weaseled out of his invitation to have a good look at myself. Instead, I listed all the super-vital reasons why *my* stress and *my* problems were so very important and unavoidable.

Dave nodded. "You know, when I feel like that, I remind myself that I'm not running for president. I have a big job, sure, but I'm not saving the world." He paused and made sure I was still listening. "Jules," he said. "You're not saving the world either."

And for some reason, just like that, the truth hit me. Dave was right. I wasn't saving the world. And somehow, that thought didn't make me feel bad or lesser than. In fact, it helped me get a handle on my anxiety.

Here's the thing: Even if your work *is* saving the world, is it worth losing yourself in the process? If you don't take care of yourself, your impact will be significantly shorter lived.

When we stop thinking that our work is "the most important thing ever," we start getting a handle on our anxiety. We begin to create a well-rounded life that we want.

When I applied my desire to the life that I wanted to live, I was successful in my career, yes, *and also* in my personal development, relationships, health, and spirituality. I became passionate about my *entire life*. That's the way to live, and it's available to all of us.

83

Buy Plants

MY EX-GIRLFRIEND deserves full credit for this tip. She's the one who introduced me to the Zen boost that bringing nature inside can give. Once I had a few living things in my space, I found my love for all living things increase.

Decorate each room in your home with at least one plant. This will add color and make your space feel both more alive and calmer. There's a peace that plants bring with them, and a quiet vibrancy, too. It's not a "jump up and down" energy but a wise, sentient feeling they bring to any environment. If you thought candles brought warmth and love to a room, wait until you try plants! They bring wisdom.

At the risk of you thinking I'm nuts, I'm also going to suggest that you try talking to your plants. This may sound a bit much for you, but consider this: Even if it's a placebo effect, talking to your plants will make you feel a sense of community—like you're not the only life-form out there. If being alone at home gives you anxiety, plants offer strong, silent company. And, if you ever feel like you're not being heard at home, know that plants hear you.

Keep this in mind, too: it's not just the plants that make your pad more Zen and peaceful but the pots or vases that they're in as well. Try some fun or pleasing color options to liven up your space (see the next tip, "Surround Yourself with Color"). And don't forget to water your new friends!

• • •

#OwnYourAnxiety tip: While you're considering how to strategically and mindfully celebrate your living space with plants, also think about creating a sacred space just for you in your home. Contemplate which colors, decorations, lighting, pictures, mementos, and/or other objects will calm you down. Remember that it's hard to be scared when we're in touch with how sacred we are. Your sacred space will serve as a reminder of this.

84

Surround Yourself with Color

AVE YOU ever felt lost in a deep appreciation for green pastures and blue skies? It's hard not to be amazed by the perfect piece of grass blowing gently in the wind or of the turquoise blue sea. During some of my most eye-twitching, chest-thumping, pits-dripping, butterflies-in-my-stomach anxiety attacks over the last ten years or so, nature's beautiful and brilliant backdrops have helped me to relax.

They say that the most trustworthy politicians always choose blue ties over red, that blue evokes calmness and trust, whereas red brings out aggression and anger. Seems crazy, right? But isn't it interesting that the sky is blue, not red? That lakes and oceans are blue, not yellow?

You and I may have our favorite colors when it comes to fashion, paint, and yoga mats, but did you know that the colors with which you surround yourself will have an impact on your anxiety? There's a direct correlation between the color of our external surroundings and our internal state. That's extremely empowering information.

For years, I've felt that the color of my surroundings influences my mood, but I didn't know that color could also lessen my anxiety. That was a massive realization and revelation. Yes, blue and green are reminiscent of nature, which can evoke feelings of peace, serenity, and beauty—all of which reduce anxiety. But did you know that, even in lab studies, lower anxiety levels are attributed to environments with blue and green tones, whereas yellow and red surroundings tend to heighten anxiety? It's not just a mental connection to these hues; it's nature. It's science.

And it's not just these two colors that have magical impact. Pink can also be calming. Imagine your life with more blue, green, and perhaps pink around you. How do you think that might make you feel?

We can't stop there. We need to keep going: What colors should we be avoiding? In addition to red and yellow, which can steal our chilled-out Zen and replace it with anxiety and nervous energy, many negative emotions are heightened by dark colors. Have you ever felt happier, more loving, and more vibrant while wearing all black? I doubt it.

Start thinking about the colors you surround yourself with so that you can also reflect on how you want to live. When it comes to skin color let's agree that all shades are beautiful, but when it comes to our homes and other spaces, here's to using colors to soothe the mind and calm the soul.

85

Keep a Memento That Calms You Down

I HAVE A TATTOO on my arm that reads, "Life is what you make of it" in old Hebrew text. I've had it for ten years, gotten sick of it never, and looked at it as a reminder countless times. There's enormous power in sayings and mantras. There's also massive strength in having a memento that calms you down.

Out of sight is out of mind. We've all seen and heard this expression before. Have you ever heard the opposite? It's equally true, if not more so.

In sight is in mind.

Keeping a talisman that calms you down is key. Always carry an object or a phrase that grounds you. Keep it close. Guard it. Look at it. Embrace it.

Remember, owning anxiety is about channeling the energy of anxiety and shifting how we view it to become empowered by it. If I'm feeling anxious and remember my tattoo, which in essence serves the same purpose as a memento, the conversation in my mind goes something like this:

Damn, I'm feeling pretty anxious. All these deadlines and commitments are getting to me. I feel overwhelmed. Ugh. My heart's racing.

Julian, remember this: Life is what you make of it. These deadlines and commitments are going to be here no matter what. Right now, this is the way it is. When the time is right I can dig deeper to evaluate where I've extended myself and possibly make lifestyle changes, but right now, I'm not breaking my word, so how do I want to show up? "Life is what you make of it." I'm going to make the most of it and channel this energy into making each of these experiences the most they can be. That's what I'm going to do.

I'm not saying you need to go out and get a tattoo. And, depending on the type of person you are, having a tattoo might work you up more than not having one in the first place! Maybe your object is a mug or a poster or a keychain that has a message of value to you. Maybe it's a small memento from a loved one. Maybe it's a photo of someone who you love deeply and it calms your nerves just to look at it. The options are endless. If you get anxious often, if you feel alone often, your little memento can be your reminder to reset, with positive self-talk, nose-to-belly (NTB) breathing, a few minutes of meditation or yoga, or whatever works to get you where you want to be.

I wear, on my pinky finger, a tree-of-life ring that I bought from a vendor in Tulum a few years back. This is a powerful memento for me. When life feels like it's getting to be too much and that I may not be able to keep up, I remember the ring and remind myself to be steady like a tree and to breathe (since trees give oxygen). I also remember that this is the tree of life, always going and growing.

86

Make Calming Friends

EVER HEAR the old adage, "You are who you hang out with"? I've definitely noticed in my own life a direct correlation between the quality of my actions and the people I'm associating with. And at times when I've thought less than favorably about myself, it's been when I'm hanging out with bad influences. Whether we like to admit it or not, we're sponges. We soak up what's around us.

Do you want to be more chilled, centered, and relaxed? Make friends with people who are calming. Doing this intentionally will empower you to find your sacred space—where anxiety is controlled and smaller than you rather than running rampant.

Several years ago, after hitting all the professional highs that I was aiming for, I realized that the life I'd worked so hard to achieve wasn't what I really wanted. Socially, I was "connected," but I wasn't calm and *connected*.

I had the same habits in different relationships.

I hung out with the same type of people in a different city. I was in the same scene in different bars.

When I looked around me, I saw that too many of my newer acquaintances and friends were drunk. I was over it. Something had to change.

I was determined to find my calm connection to the physical world and to the metaphysical universe. I knew I needed different people in my life, positive role models to take me where I wanted to go. I decided it was time to be intentional about who I hung out with.

**When the student is ready,
the teacher appears.**

Through an interesting turn of events, I met two of the biggest influences in my life—Rabbi Jacobs and my yoga teacher Aryan—within a two-month timeframe. You can imagine what this did for me, right? Suddenly, my attempts to forget my anxiety by partying until 4 a.m. were replaced with me doing some real learning with learned people. I observed the Sabbath. I spent days in a yoga studio. And I felt great.

Some of my friends didn't get it. But some of my other friends had discovered this path on their own and inspired me to join them. I've done the same for others, too, and *this* is how we find our tribe. *This* is how we connect to our best self. *This* is how we evolve. *This* is how we own anxiety.

87

Thank Something
Bigger Than You

NOT ALL habits are bad. There's absolutely nothing wrong with a habit . . . if it's a good one. A good habit is anything that makes you a better version of yourself. A bad habit takes you away from being the best version of yourself.

Habits that cause you to eat better, live healthier, treat people kinder—these are all good. No need to change something that's working, right? And if you're someone who habitually practices gratitude, hooray to you. Please keep it up. Thanking something bigger than yourself can have a humbling and settling effect. It doesn't matter what you believe in—some people refer to the Higher Power, the Creator, the Source, the Universe. It's not what you call it that matters but that you will feel connected by speaking to the source. Like you're in sync, moving through life with a bit of help.

When we thank something bigger, we never walk alone. We're connected to the biggest being out there. Just feeling that connection helps our fears go away and opens endless possibilities. In this state of possibilities, anxiety shrivels. We feel more whole, more complete. We can discover more meaning in our lives.

A wise spiritual leader once said to me that if I could walk holding on to the Higher Power's hand, I would always feel connected. I like to think of that image when anxiety takes hold of me. I let go of anxiety and grasp the hand of the Higher Power. I know it will take me where I need to go, without a care or worry in the world.

Now, check this out: It doesn't need to be the Higher Power's hand. Thanking something bigger than you is vast, open, limitless. There is literally so much to thank. How frigging incredible is that?

We can thank Mother Nature every time we take a bite of food. We can thank the air for giving us the oxygen we need to breathe. We can thank the trees for reminding us of the natural beauty all around, the mountains for reminding us that we are so small and that our problems are trivial compared with the wondrous planet that we are blessed to be living on. We can thank mentors who have passed on, and remember that if we close our eyes and dig deep enough within while letting our soul connect above, we can feel guided and loved.

It's not so much what you thank, it's that you remember, during high anxiety-moments, confusion, and chaos, that you can connect, reflect, and step forward.

88

Spread Love

THE OTHER day, I was in the midst of a challenging workout at the gym. I was gasping because of the exertion and trying to maintain my mental focus by breathing loudly, in and out. I was definitely in the zone.

Into the gym walked this guy about my age. He was slouched over, dragging his feet as he walked. I noticed that his arms were crossed. I gave him a big smile and between gasps for air said, "Hi! Good morning!"

"Hi, good morning," he said back, quietly, then he went to the cardio area and stood on a treadmill. He just stood there, looking out the window, arms crossed, treadmill off.

I carried on with my workout. About ten minutes went by. But, in the mirrors of the gym, I noticed the guy was *still* just standing there, not moving, treadmill off. It was weird, but I didn't think too much of it. I finished my workout and left. Then, a few days later, I was working out again, and in walked the same guy. He went straight to the treadmill and just stood on it for twenty minutes, again without turning it on.

Maybe he just comes here to pretend he's working out so he can tell his partner he "went to the gym"? It was a crazy thought, but I was starting to wonder. Through the mirrors, I took another look at the man. He looked sad, confused, and alone. A voice in my head said, *Julian, this is not your business. You do you. Finish your workout.* But for some reason, I decided not to listen to that voice.

I walked over to the guy and said hello.

"Hi," he said.

"Listen, I'm not trying to pry, but I'm kind of wondering: What are you working on today?"

"I'm planning on doing some cardio," he answered. "But sometimes I have a really hard time finding the determination to move. I force myself into the gym at least a few days a week regardless."

Wow. As soon as I heard that, I had so much respect for this man. First, he was so truthful. He took this huge risk to be vulnerable with me, a total stranger, about what he was doing and the struggle he was having. Beyond that, he was also full of courage and tenacity. He showed up, no matter what, even if he didn't have the strength to turn on the equipment.

"You know what?" I replied. "I get it completely. Sometimes I can't even show up to the gym at all. I don't even make it as far as you have today, so kudos to you."

He nodded. Then I saw a little smile creep up the corners of his mouth.

I wished him luck and he wished the same for me.

Shortly after our brief conversation, he turned on the treadmill. Then he started to move! After twenty minutes, he moved to the elliptical machine. Shortly after, another man walked into the gym. I offered him a morning greeting. Then my new friend, still on the elliptical, called out, "Hello!" to the new guy. And just like that, we were a community of people vulnerably living life, working through our challenges as we worked out together. And to think that my inner voice almost convinced me to tune out. Our inner voice can lead us wildly astray sometimes.

I realized in this moment that spreading love is truly a contagious act and one that we should take upon ourselves even when it feels a bit weird. When you share kindness and love with others—even in the subtlest ways—people will go on to share love with others. And so love and kindness spreads, for the good of all. This is what we do. We humans can spread love. And when we do, we feel the power of the good deed. We carry our heads a little higher, and our hearts brim with a lot more love. It's in this beautiful state that anxiety loses its power and loving kindness wins.

Who are the people you see regularly to whom you can spread love?

Who are the people you don't even know that you can spread love to?

Spreading love is truly a contagious act.

• • • • • • • • • •

89

Talk About It

THE MOST obvious things to do are those that we do the least. For so long, I put out into the world a false version of myself as invincible. I thought that to be successful, I needed to mask my emotions—especially vulnerability.

During the first few years of Notable, I spent most of my time behind closed doors, ideating and building up the company. I was by myself in my struggle. And it was then that I became an anxious person. I became truly afraid of the unknown. How would I pay for lunch or for rent? I partied to forget, then came home to find anxiety, stress, and depression waiting for me. When I was out in the world, I acted like everything was perfect even though I knew that it wasn't. If only I'd been willing to talk about it. But I wasn't.

Years later, I became open to talking about my challenges. From there, I put myself in a place of growth and renewal. From there, I healed.

Today, I speak openly about my anxiety. I speak about it with great pride. Pride? "How can I be proud of anxiety?" you may ask.

Think of it this way:

- We shine light into darkness when we speak openly about our challenges.

- When we accept teaching, advice, and mentorship from others, shame turns into pride.

- When we admit who we are and what we're going through to people, they're more likely to embrace us. Shame disappears. Pride prevails.

These days, when I give workshops on anxiety, I fully share how my eye twitches like mad when anxiety gets to me, how I feel nervous when I speak but do it anyway, how my heart races, and how I deal with that. I'm proud to talk freely about debilitating anxiety attacks—because I've had them, and now, I'm doing much better without them. And if they come back, then I'll still keep talking about them, because there's nothing to be ashamed of, and I'm not alone. It's an important message, one I want everyone to understand!

There's so much power in talking about what we're *growing* through. All we need to do is believe in the process of change, embrace it, and own it.

90

Volunteer

ONE OF the best-kept mental health secrets is volunteering. By giving a little, you get a lot. The secret is now out of the bag!

People volunteer for several reasons—to help with a cause they're passionate about; to remember a loved one who passed on; to network for business; to socialize. Some do it as a chance to learn and gain experience. Whatever the reason you do it, volunteering will help you own your anxiety. It improves your feelings of self-worth and shows us that most of our petty worries are insignificant compared with what others, all over the world, are dealing with.

Give back to those in need. Doing so drastically minimizes anxiety while maximizing positive feelings such as empathy and belonging. For years, I went through life thinking that I was far too busy to give back. I used to put it off, telling myself that when I made more money and had more time, I'd volunteer. I'm sure some of you have also felt the same way. But it's worth making the time now rather than later—not only because the world needs more giving people like you to help fix it, but also because your mental health will improve.

Luckily, I discovered the importance of volunteering about ten years ago, and I haven't stopped since. I learned about a brilliant charity called NABS—the National Advertising Benevolent Society. NABS helps people in the advertising and communications industry, offering emotional support, financial aid after job loss, and many other needed resources. I felt a connection to the mission of NABS because I was becoming intimately aware of how a couple of wrong moves can put you in a very tough spot. This fear would often keep me up at night. So I passionately joined the board, where I remained for several years.

Are you ready to give a little and get a lot? Then start thinking about a cause you care about, send an email, and start sharing your amazing skills with the world. Here are some tips to make volunteering work for you:

Don't overcommit. It's easy to take on too much. Do only what you can and don't commit to more than that. If you do, volunteering can have a reverse impact on your anxiety and begin to create it. So, like anything in life that you take on, put comfortable parameters on the commitment.

Choose an initiative that you're passionate about. When it comes to your career, it's easy to get stuck in a job that offers an adequate salary, decent work-life balance, and benefits, rather than one you just can't wait to start each day. Volunteering is a way to dream big. Volunteer for a cause that you deeply care about. That will get you going every day!

Know who else is volunteering. If you don't like the group that your volunteering with, you're probably not going to like volunteering. So make sure that you enjoy the time with your co-volunteers.

91

Let the Truth
Set You Free

YOU'VE HEARD it before. And it's true. The truth will set you free. When we're hiding something, anxiety races and takes over. Truth heals. Truth lets us release the baggage we've been holding. We've all done, thought, and said things that we know are out of alignment with our better self. Too many people are walking around holding on to this. With shame. Bottling up shame leads to a spiral of negative thoughts and self-inflicted, deep emotional pain that can move into our entire being.

And it doesn't need to be this way. There is freedom in the truth. It's a freedom that you deserve. We all do. Big, small, or medium. I invite you to let it go.

Let go of shame. It's too heavy to carry.

Years ago, when I was living in Tel Aviv and studying yoga, my instructor Aryan would ease his way into yoga poses and postures instinctively. Being a flexible person, I'd try to do the same. A proper yoga pose remains engaged. Present. Active. But my poses weren't like Aryan's. They were butchered, choppy.

Aryan was patient. He taught me how to release my body into a pose, to ease into it, and to get to know my own body in space—and to enjoy it. I learned to be truthful about my journey, with less ego.

As I heightened my practice, I started to understand that while every pose required control, it also required surrender.

So I ask the questions:

What can you control? Control requires strength.

What can you release? Release requires faith.

Yoga is a metaphor for life. A pose is a moment of truth. To be true to a pose, release what you're hiding and have the strength to truthfully admit it.

To be true to where you are in your life, stop holding on so tightly to what you wish was and accept what is. Stop holding on to what you did and, with pride and excitement, own what you will do. From this place of acceptance, the opportunity to proactively evolve becomes fully possible. The first step to owning your anxiety is accepting it. Accept why you have it, and analyze your entire life so that you can see where your anxiety originates. Talk about it with yourself or with someone you trust. And then accept this truth and commit to growing from it.

I accept you. Now it is time for *you* to accept you.

92

Share Your Journey with Others

WHEN WE give, we grow. And giving can take many forms. In a previous tip, we talked about giving our time to a charity. But that's just one form of sharing. We can also share our experiences—especially with those who need guidance or a sense of belonging.

So much anxiety comes from fear of the unknown or fear of being alone. When we share our knowledge, we build trust and community. We create a group of like-minded people around us who can guide us on our journeys and give us a sense that we're being accompanied. Also, others in your midst might see things that you don't and offer some good advice.

When we share, we feel better about ourselves because we self-reflect and are encouraged to trust others. We feel more confident when we help others, and we feel grounded when we receive guidance that we really need. This makes us happy and evokes positive self-talk, which, as you know, has been proven to help us take ownership of our anxiety. Remember tip 52 dedicated to positive self-talk? This is what the pro athletes do before they get their game on, and if it works for LeBron, it'll work for us.

I've tried to turn sharing into a regular habit. I'm always amazed and grateful when others do the same for me. During tax season, my father, who is normally very calm, goes into high gear. But even so, I've seen him turn it all off and share with me a life story that quickly relaxes both of us. I've watched my mother, during her bout with cancer, go from worried to chilled out and in control just by sharing lessons she's learned from her ordeal. And I've watched myself go from a state of anxiety to a state of centered calm by sharing my truth.

Who might you be able to share with? Perhaps you have a friend who would truly benefit from your story? I bet you that there's a local community group that would deeply appreciate it. Sharing isn't just verbal, either. Maybe you have it in you to share more of your story, authentically and vulnerably, at same time judiciously, with your social media network—care to give that a shot? Another thing you may consider is simply writing more. Try it! You may have an uplifting release just by writing. By doing that you're in essence sharing with the Universe, even if nobody else sees it. Crazy, right? But it's possible. Anything is possible.

To give is to get. When we give, we often get in return more than we ever imagined possible.

93

Take Time
Daily to Re-Center

AMID CHAOS, we can find calm. During an anxious episode, we can take a step back. In dark, there is light. In fury, there's might. In fear exists love. In despair, we still have air. Yet we forget. There's a lot going on around us all the time. We have families, commitments, and obligations. The duties never seem to end.

And there's a lot going on inside us, too. Every moment, we're changing. Our bodies and minds never stop. Even while we sleep—that is, if we're lucky enough to get quality shut-eye—internally, we're in a state of constant change.

In our nonstop world, sometimes all we need is a pause button. But it's hard to find. At times, it feels like the world looks down upon those who seek a pause. Why can't we just push that button once in a while? Since when does taking a break mean that we're weak and incapable? Who says that high achievers can't also slow down?

Grateful should we all be for the conscious movement of meditation centers, yoga studios, healers, and light-workers emerging in our busy cities and less busy towns. I'm so stoked by the number of yoga mats I see accompanying professionally dressed people as they commute to work or ride the elevator up to the office. There's an awakening happening in our communities and it's mindful and beautiful.

Yet, so many of us still feel like we're just treading water to stay afloat. How will we ever find time and space to hit the pause button? How will we feel centered? It won't happen unless we intentionally find that button and push it. Every single day.

Here's how to re-center:

Step 1: Find a quiet space. This is easier than you think, and it doesn't need to be perfectly quiet. It can be quietish. Think: a private room at home, your car, an empty coffee shop.

Step 2: Close your eyes. It's key to feeling safe in your quiet space.

Step 3: Breathe with your eyes closed, inhaling through your nose. Direct deep, luxurious breaths intentionally to your belly so that it expands. (Remember the NTB breath from tip 1, "Breathe.")

Step 4: Smile. Let your cheeks make their way toward your ears. Enjoy this moment of re-centering as it takes over your being.

The more centered you are the more manageable your anxiety will be.

94

Get More Sun

AS I WRITE this, it's below zero degrees where I live. But the sun is out and the sky is blue. As I was leaving home this morning, I decided to take a few minutes to enjoy the weather. *Enjoy the weather?* That may sound crazy to you. I *am* a little crazy—about enjoying life. I'm crazy about strategies that will make me feel better. I'm crazy about easing anxiety and knowing how to own it when it does show up.

Sunlight burns anxiety away. The serotonin boost from the sun gives us a happiness lift. Plus, if you're someone who suffers from SAD (Seasonal Affective Disorder), you have even more reason to get yourself into that sun. The happier you are, the less anxious you'll be. And, if you're still anxious while you're happy, it's never quite as bad as being anxious while you're sad. Bask in that for a minute.

We've all heard about the negative effects of too much sun exposure, so let's not go overboard here. I'm not suggesting tanning for eight hours a day without wearing sunscreen. But do try to get out in that sun for at least a few minutes a day, if you can. Apart from serotonin, you'll also be taking in vitamin D from the sun's rays, which offers myriad health benefits, such as increased absorption of calcium, which is key for promoting bone growth. Vitamin D is also linked to immune function and helps promote resistance against certain diseases.

Hope it's a bright day for you. Let's soak it up.

. . .

#OwnYourAnxiety tip: If you're living in a dark winter climate, you can still do many things, and you're as much a part of our movement as anyone else, so don't ever forget that. Get outside for a walk during the daylight every day, use full-spectrum lights, and, hey, light lots of candles for your space(s). Owning anxiety is a holistic game, so let's think about it in a 360-degree way.

Sunlight burns anxiety away.

. . . .

95

Manage Your Breaks

ARE YOU mindful of what you're doing or not doing on your breaks? A break from work or from your parental responsibilities is so important. When we don't take a break, we exhaust ourselves. Anxiety comes knocking shortly thereafter.

Let me give you an example. Just the other day, I was in a cute Italian café. At the table across from me a woman sat down. She had an espresso, which she slammed back in two sips and then proceeded to feverishly type away on her phone. One of her legs was shaking convulsively. Fifteen minutes later, this woman looked far more anxious as she left the café than she had when she arrived. So was this her break?

Beside me a man sat down with a gigantic latte. He was head-down in his coffee and then head-down on his phone. He grunted under his breath. Then his phone rang.

"Hello, Joe Smith, here! Oh, yes, let me write that down. Hang on... going to type it into my phone as I put you on speaker. Ugh, it's a little loud in here. Sorry, can you speak up? Speak up, I said!" He shouted this. I watched as his knee started to shake, up, down, up, down. A few moments later, he ended the call, chugged the latte, and rushed out of the café.

Do you see how both these people didn't really break effectively? All that they did was exchange one anxiety-provoking activity for another. To make it even worse, they were consuming caffeine.

If we don't think about how we take a break, we may eventually break. Tune in to yourself. What does your body or mind want most right now?

- If it wants to feel invigorated, go for a walk.

- If it wants to feel centered and calm, close your eyes and meditate.

- If it wants to feel energized, do some pushups or jumping jacks.

- If it needs a charge of energy, opt for a shot of ginger instead of caffeine.

- If it's hungry, eat a healthy snack, like a green apple, not something full of processed sugar or heavy carbs.

- If it needs a break from reality and an escape, read something that takes you there.

Tune out the world. There's no reason to be hooked on a screen on your break. Why go from your laptop screen to your mobile screen? Put your cell on silent and disconnect for a few minutes. You earned it.

I'd also suggest giving yourself at least three deep, intentional breaths of gratitude on your break (see tip 67, "Give Gratitude"). You have so much to be grateful for. A break is the perfect time to remind yourself of that. The more intentional we are about our breaks, the less chance there is that we'll ever break.

96

Don't Jaywalk

ONE SUNNY afternoon, after hours of yoga training, Aryan and I were walking through bustling downtown Tel Aviv to get a healthy lunch. We were feeling so Zen but we were also starving.

We approached a busy street, and no cars were coming, so I said, "Aryan, let's cross."

He looked at me with a tilted head. "Julian, when I feel good, I like to continue that for as long as I can. If we cross against the lights, that feeling may change. Why risk that?"

And just like that, he shifted the way I looked at anxiety.

With so many external things that we can't control, why not intentionally control what we can? Jaywalking might have shaved a few seconds off our walk, but it would have ruined our hard-earned internal calm.

If you're in a Zen state, stay there! Don't do anything that will whisk you away from a state of grace. Be present. Breathe. Give gratitude. Savor the moment, especially if you're in a conversation with a great person. And, if that person is you, the same applies, because you're amazing!

97

Watch the Sun Rise and Set

HAVE YOU ever seen a sunrise? There's something so calming and inspiring about it. I feel most aware of the blessing of a new day when I see the sun come up.

In yoga, for thousands of years the yogis have been starting their practice with sun salutations, and these are the least anxious people around. I think there's good reason here, because when we connect with the sun we gain comfort, assurance, and power. Even the thought of the sun warms us up. Right?

You may be thinking, "Julian, sounds nice. I also love a sunrise, but I see one once every few years if I'm lucky!" Here's the good news: You can wake up with the sunrise without even looking outside. Try putting a gorgeous photo or painting of the sunrise on a wall where you will see it first thing every morning.

And, if you want the real thing and have access to it, that's great. Try going to bed early and rising early. Even on a cloudy, dark day, the sun still rises. And on a bright, cloudless day, it rises as a gorgeous, life-affirming spectacle. You'll find an inner sense of calm and serenity for this natural wonder. You might even connect to the source of creation.

The same goes for sunsets. Wherever you are, try to catch the sun going down. Take a moment to appreciate what you're seeing, whether that's on a cold winter day or a gorgeous summer evening. And remember to engage with the sunset. Be grateful for the moment. What a gift! Sunsets are one of the most vivid displays of natural beauty in the entire world, so I *really* encourage you to engage with them more often. Make it a goal.

I've been in minus-twenty-degree weather driving home from a long day of work and caught a gorgeous glimpse of the sun. I could have stayed behind the wheel and felt jealous of someone who posted a sunset pic from a warm tropical destination, but seeing a sunset in the car on a frigid day is an opportunity to pull over and appreciate it too. And, if you're walking, I invite you to stop and appreciate those divine colors for a few minutes! You'll never be sorry for appreciating life. The sunset is available to everyone. Virtually anywhere. More action and less excuses. Why? Because as the sun goes down, so will your anxiety.

98

Help Others

D O YOU know the biblical story of Esther? Esther is married to a very tough king, who has an advisor named Haman with a dark idea of wiping out all of the Jews from the land. Esther is a Jew herself, and although she knows she'll be spared because she's the king's wife, she worries for her people. She decides to alert the king immediately, even though *nobody*, including the wife of the king, may approach him uninvited. Esther puts her life on the line for the sake of the greater good. And in the end, she succeeds in saving the Jewish people.

When we help others, we go from filling our own basic needs to fulfilling someone else's needs. Is there anything more intimate and inspiring than that?

"But I'm way, way, way too busy to help someone else."

"I can't afford to give to a charity now."

"I'm beyond anxious and stressed out with my own crap, so how can I deal with someone else's?"

I confess I've thought all these things at some point, and I now see them as my justifications to wallow in stasis. To make excuses. To be comfortable with not growing even though I know all too well that a life without growth is a life of decay and decline.

Here is the truth: Helping others offers *huge* benefits to the giver, not just to the receiver. Some studies even suggest that when it comes to giving, both the giver and the receiver of help experience a reduction of stress responses.

We're talking about much more than gift-giving here. When you give to others, when you volunteer for a cause, when you spend time with those less fortunate, you grow and your anxiety dissipates. So what's the big takeaway?

Listen to your altruistic side.

Go and help, and allow the great benefits to enter your life. By giving, you will be less stressed. By being less stressed, you will have less anxiety. By lessening your anxiety, you'll feel better. What's more? You will feel full of self-worth and your heart will be bursting. Give a little, get a lot.

99

Embrace Where You're At

DIFFERENT MOMENTS in our lives require different kinds of focus. Often, anxiety stems from trying to do too many things at once. We become overwhelmed, then the negative self-talk kicks in, because we feel we've fallen short of accomplishing the many things that we're desperately trying to achieve. This spiral causes major anxiety. It can also cause us to miss out on the very thing we want and need most—in my case, it was love.

I spent the majority of my twenties obsessed with my career and financial growth. When I was thinking about quitting my sought-after job in Silicon Valley and leaving my amazing life in San Francisco to start my own business, I remember staring myself down in the mirror. I asked myself, "Julian, if you put everything you have into building your own company and you give up the majority of your twenties to pursue it, will you be successful and happy by the time you're thirty?" The answer was clear: It was yes.

But what I didn't understand then is that I didn't fully own my decision. I wasn't totally comfortable giving up everything in pursuit of "career success." I kept trying to squeeze in meaningful romantic relationships, but they weren't working. I was trying to do and be and achieve everything, but I was coming up short. My inadequacy showed up in the form of arguments, insecurities, and ultimately breakups. I caused way too much drama and anxiety. I can't blame myself for wanting love. But looking back, I certainly see how I wasn't clearly deciding what I wanted and what I was prepared to sacrifice to get it.

A few years ago, I hopped on a call with Rabbi Jacobs to do a little "life check" with him. He asked me what I was focusing on at age thirty-three.

I paused. I knew what was coming.

Know and embrace the moment of life you're in and where you're focused.

• • • • • • • • •

"Julian," he said. "You've spent most of your adult life focused on work. Can you afford to focus properly on love now? If not now, when?"

I understood what he was saying. And I knew he was right.

The big lesson here is to know and embrace the moment of life you're in and where you're focused. If you try to do it all, it won't work. You can't fit in a sweet yoga practice in the morning, work twelve hours, spend an hour mentoring your colleagues, hit the gym for two hours, and play with your kids for four hours every day, plus get nine hours of sleep every night. You also can't become the world's best partner if you're not ready to be all-in with the relationship. You can't achieve washboard abs (not saying you should want that) if you're giving in to your pizza addiction every day. You're not going to be able to afford your dream mansion if you can't follow through with something that will yield enough income to gather the down payment. If you want to find peace and experience an anxiety-owned existence, your intentions and your actions have to sync up.

Be aligned.

The you that you are being and the you that you want to be are not aligned if you say one thing and do another. Focus on what matters most in your life now. Align your actions so they're clear and powerful. If you don't, you're signing up for anxiety and misery, and no one wants that.

You get the idea, right? To own your anxiety, know what stage of your life you're in and embrace that, aligning your actions accordingly. Say goodbye to anxiety and hello to walking with your head held high with the truth.

Growing Together

YOU DID it. You finished all 99 ways to own your anxiety. Let's take a moment of silence.

Let's take a juicy NTB breath.

You're invited to join the thousands of others around the world who are also owning their anxiety. As you do, take a soothing, grounding breath through your nose and down to your belly and give yourself a special moment to reflect on this life-changing accomplishment.

Allow yourself to enjoy deeply the feeling of gratitude that is yours to embody. And if you're not feeling particularly grateful, try getting a little more intentional:

Take a deep breath of gratitude, from your nose to your belly. As the belly expands with delicious air, say to yourself, "Grateful am I for," and once you reach the maximum of a deep, deep inhale, finish the statement with "my dedication to myself." Very slowly, share your air with the universe.

I am so proud of you.

You've gone through this book like the incredible human that you are. You challenged your less evolved self to become your higher self. You went deep within so that you could become more evolved without needing anything but you. The you who needs nothing more than what you already have. What you already are. What you've always been. *Perfection.*

We often get a bit lost along the road of life. We fall out of alignment. Our path deviates from straight to jagged. We create bad habits and we stop listening to what our bodies, minds, and souls are trying to tell us. We silence the all-knowing voice that combines intuition and our internal (eternal) compass, as the louder, more conscious voice becomes fixated on our external desires. But not anymore. You see, now you know. Now you are armed. You are ready to continue your journey of evolvement, and I couldn't be readier for you.

By now you're walking and talking to yourself and others differently. You're eating and drinking differently. You're moving and prioritizing differently. You're still you and I'm glad about that, because you were incredible and you still are, only you are now a heck of a lot wiser.

Thank you for being a part of this journey. Thank you for trusting me with your time.

Thank you. Thank you. Thank you! I'm so grateful for you.

I invite you to continue on the journey of growth with me. Join me on JulianBrass.com, OwnYourAnxiety.com, on insta, and most of all make sure to sign up for my daily Life Letter. It's a brief piece of inspirational writing that I send out every morning to people all over the world who are dedicated to being their best selves.

On my site, you'll also learn about my one-on-one coaching, online courses, in-person workshops, retreats, and corporate sessions.

This is just the beginning, my friends. Stay connected with me and let's continue to grow, *together*.

With love, light, respect, and gratitude,

JULIAN
#OwnYourAnxiety

Notes

1 BREATHE

breath rates and life spans: See Harshad Rajandekar, "The Curious Connection between Breath Rate and Longevity," *Dr. Herbz*, April 28, 2016, https://drherbz.wordpress.com/2016/04/28/the-curious-connection-between-breath-rate-and-longevity/.

parasympathetic nervous system: See "Step 4: Practice Your Breathing Skills," Anxieties.com, accessed May 21, 2019, https://www.anxieties.com/57/panic-step4#.XN2DBVNKhE5.

2 SMILE MORE

Science suggests: See, for example, Jingjing Chang et al., "When You Smile You Become Happy: Evidence from Resting State Task-Based fMRI," *Biological Psychology* 103 (December 2014): 100–6, https://doi.org/10.1016/j.biopsycho.2014.08.003.

4 SWIM

"vigorous exercise like swimming": Aimee C. Kimball quoted in Therese J. Borchard, "Just Keep Swimming: How Swimming Reduces Depression," *Beyond Blue*, Beliefnet, accessed May 21, 2019, https://www.beliefnet.com/columnists/beyondblue/2010/07/just-keep-swimming-how-swimmin.html.

5 QUIT OR REDUCE COFFEE

"a chemical substance": ScienceDaily, s.v. "Psychoactive drug," accessed May 20, 2019, https://www.sciencedaily.com/terms/psychoactive_drug.htm.

most commonly used psychoactive drug: Roberto Corti et al., "Coffee Acutely Increases Sympathetic Nerve Activity and Blood Pressure Independently of Caffeine Content: Role of Habitual Versus Nonhabitual Drinking," *Circulation* 106 (December 3, 2002): 2935–40, https://doi.org/10.1161/01.CIR.0000046228.97025.3A.

The American Psychiatric Association named: In the *Diagnostic and Statistical Manual of Mental Disorders*. See Encyclopedia of Mental Disorders, s.v. "Caffeine-related disorders," accessed May 20, 2019, http://www.minddisorders.com/Br-Del/Caffeine-related-disorders.html.
one study showed: See "Is That Guy Threatening You? Or Is It That Extra Cup of Coffee?" *The Scicurious Brain, Scientific American*, July 23, 2012, https://blogs.scientificamerican.com/scicurious-brain/is-that-guy-threatening-you-or-is-it-that-extra-cup-of-coffee/.

9 HUG AND CUDDLE MORE
Oxytocin is known to have: Markus MacGill, "What Is the Link between Love and Oxytocin?" MedicalNewsToday, updated September 4, 2017, https://www.medicalnewstoday.com/articles/275795.php.

11 GET A MASSAGE
In a recent randomized study: See Lecia Bushak, "Therapeutic Massage for Anxiety: How Touch Therapy Improves Mental Health," *Vitality*, Medical Daily, August 4, 2016, https://www.medicaldaily.com/therapeutic-massage-anxiety-how-touch-therapy-improves-mental-health-393837.

13 DRINK MORE WATER
Our brains are mostly water... flushes toxins from our bodies: Na Zhang et al., "Effect of Water Supplementation on Cognitive Performances and Mood among Male College Students in Cangzhou, China: Study Protocol of a Randomized Controlled Trial," *International Journal of Environmental Research and Public Health* 14, no. 9 (August 27, 2017): 966, https://doi.org/10.3390/ijerph14090966.

15 PLAY
According to an article... the *pet effect*: Steven Feldman, "Alleviating Anxiety, Stress and Depression with the Pet Effect," Anxiety and Depression Association of America, accessed May 21, 2019, https://adaa.org/learn-from-us/from-the-experts/blog-posts/consumer/alleviating-anxiety-stress-and-depression-pet.

16 SING OUT LOUD
Researchers from the University of East Anglia: Tom Shakespeare and Alice Whieldon, "Sing Your Heart Out: Community Singing as Part of Mental Health Recovery," *Medical Humanities* 44 (2018): 153–7, https://doi.org/10.1136/medhum-2017-011195.

Research has shown: Gunter Kreutz et al., "Effects of Choir Singing or Listening on Secretory Immunoglobulin A, Cortisol, and Emotional State," *Journal of Behavioral Medicine* 27, no. 6 (December 2004): 623–35, https://doi.org/10.1007/s10865-004-0006-9.

the louder the better: See, for example, "How to Stimulate Your Vagus Nerve for Better Mental Health," SASS—Student Academic Success Service, University of Ottawa, January 21, 2017, https://sass.uottawa.ca/sites/sass.uottawa.ca/files/how_to_stimulate_your_vagus_nerve_for_better_mental_health_1.pdf.

17 GET "SCENTUAL"

reduce anxiety in cancer patients receiving treatments: William H. Redd et al., "Fragrance Administration to Reduce Anxiety during MR Imaging," *Journal of Magnetic Resonance Imaging* 4, no. 4 (July/August 1994): 623–6, https://doi.org/10.1002/jmri.1880040419.

used in dentist offices to lower people's stress levels: Johann Lehrner et al., "Ambient Odors of Orange and Lavender Reduce Anxiety and Improve Mood in a Dental Office," *Psychology & Behavior* 86, nos. 1 and 2 (September 15, 2005): 92–5, https://doi.org/10.1016/j.physbeh.2005.06.031.

18 TAKE WARM SHOWERS OR BATHS

Warm showers are linked to that great "love hormone": Madeline Haller, "The Surprising Benefit to a Hot Shower," *Men's Health*, March 7, 2012, https://www.menshealth.com/health/a19529070/the-surprising-benefit-to-a-hot-shower/.

20 MOVE YOUR BODY

Other benefits of movement . . . age better: See, for example, Ashish Sharma, Vishal Madaan, and Frederick D. Petty, "Exercise for Mental Health," *The Primary Care Companion to the Journal of Clinical Psychiatry* 8, no. 2 (2006): 106, https://doi.org/10.4088/PCC.v08n0208a; and "Exercise for Stress and Anxiety," Anxiety and Depression Association of America, accessed May 21, 2019, https://adaa.org/living-with-anxiety/managing-anxiety/exercise-stress-and-anxiety#.

21 DANCE

prescribing dance movement therapy: Iris Bräuninger, "It Can Help Substance Abuse, PTSD, Shyness, and More," Anixety.org, October 2, 2016, https://www.anxiety.org/what-is-dance-movement-therapy.

Research has proven: See Dina Adam, Ayiesah Ramli, and Suzana Shahar, "Effectiveness of a Combined Dance and Relaxation Intervention on Reducing Anxiety and Depression and Improving Quality of Life among the Cognitively Impaired Elderly," *Sultan Qaboos University Medical Journal* 16, no. 1 (2016): 47–53, https://doi.org/10.18295/squmj.2016.16.01.009.

25 **LAUGH MORE OFTEN**
shown to help cancer patients: S.H. Kim, Y.H. Kim, H.J. Kim, "Laughter and Stress Relief in Cancer Patients: A Pilot Study," *Evidence-Based Complementary and Alternative Medicine* (May 24, 2015): 1–6, http://dx.doi.org/10.1155/2015/864739.

31 **EAT CALMING FOODS**
high-fat and low-sugar diets: See, for example, "Generalized Anxiety Disorder: Foods That Help Anxiety," The Center for Treatment of Anxiety and Mood Disorders, accessed May 21, 2019, https://centerforanxietydisorders.com/generalized-anxiety-disorder-foods-that-help-anxiety/.
Multiple scientific research findings: See, for example, Robert J. Hedaya, "Vitamin B_{12}: What Is a Vitamin B_{12} deficiency?" *Psychology Today*, February 2, 2012, https://www.psychologytoday.com/ca/blog/health-matters/201202/vitamin-b12.
Studies have shown that: See, for example, David Benton and Richard Cook, "The Impact of Selenium Supplementation on Mood," *Biological Psychiatry* 29, no. 11 (June 1991): 1092–8. https://doi.org/10.1016/0006-3223(91)90251-G.

35 **ORGANIZE YOUR LIFE**
organization is good for your mental health: See, for example, Darby E. Saxbe and Rena Repetti, "No Place like Home: Home Tours Correlate with Daily Patterns of Mood and Cortisol," *Personality and Social Psychology Bulletin* 36, no. 1 (January 2010): 71–81, https://doi.org/10.1177/0146167209352864.
A research report . . . a romantic environment: WBA Research, "Bedroom Poll: Summary of Findings," National Sleep Foundation, accessed May 21, 2019, https://www.sleepfoundation.org/sites/default/files/inline-files/NSF_Bedroom_Poll_Report.pdf.

39 PUT YOUR PHONE ON SILENT

An interesting experiment: See "Excessive Cellphone Use May Cause Anxiety, Experts Warn," ABC News, July 28, 2017, https://abcnews .go.com/Lifestyle/excessive-cellphone-anxiety-experts-warn/ story?id=48842476.

43 KEEP YOUR PHONE AWAY FROM YOUR BED

Sleep deprivation is another leading trigger of anxiety: Andrea N. Goldstein-Piekarski et al., "Sex, Sleep Deprivation, and the Anxious Brain," *Journal of Cognitive Neuroscience* 30, no. 4 (April 2018): 565–78, https://doi.org/10.1162/jocn_a_01225.

52 CONTROL YOUR SELF-TALK

This has been shown . . . absolute best: Antonis Hatzigeorgiadis and Stuart J.H. Biddle, "Negative Self-Talk during Sport Performance: Relationships with Pre-Competition Anxiety and Goal-Performance Discrepancies," *Journal of Sport Behavior* 31, no. 3 (September 2008): 237–53.

54 READ

Mindlab International . . . state of mind: See "Reading 'Can Help Reduce Stress,'" *Health News, Telegraph*, March 30, 2009, https://www .telegraph.co.uk/news/health/news/5070874/Reading-can-help-reduce-stress.html.

Reading inspires us to learn: See Keith Oatley, "Why Fiction Is Good for You: Forget Moral Edification: Psychological Research Shows Literature's Mind-Altering Effects," *Literary Review of Canada*, July/August 2011, https://reviewcanada.ca/magazine/2011/07/why-fiction-is-good-for-you/.

55 DON'T WATCH THE NEWS

A report: See Moran Bodas et al., "Anxiety-Inducing Media: The Effect of Constant News Broadcasting on the Well-Being of Israeli Television Viewers," *Psychiatry Interpersonal and Biological Processes* 78, no. 3 (September 2015): 265–76, https://doi.org/10.1080/00332747.2015 .1069658.

56 SAVE THE DATE

Science has proven: See, for example, Jaap M.J. Murre and Joeri Dros, "Replication and Analysis of Ebbinghaus' Forgetting Curve," *PLoS ONE* 10, no. 7 (July 6, 2015): e0120644, https://doi.org/10.1371/journal .pone.0120644.

58 COMPARTMENTALIZE YOUR THOUGHTS
Dale Carnegie ... minds and bodies: Dale Carnegie, *How to Stop Worrying and Start Living: Time-Tested Methods for Conquering Worry* (New York: Simon & Schuster, 1984).

59 DECIDE WHEN TO DECIDE
Research out of UC Berkeley: Yasmin Anwar, "Anxious People Are More Apt to Make Bad Decisions amid Uncertainty," *Mind & Body, Research, Berkeley News*, March 2, 2015, https://news.berkeley.edu/2015/03/02/anxious-people-decisions/.

64 LIMIT SOCIAL MEDIA USE
approximately 30 percent of the population: Sarah Fader, "Social Media Obsession and Anxiety," Anxiety and Depression Association of America, November 2018, https://adaa.org/social-media-obsession.

68 CULTIVATE QUALITY RELATIONSHIPS
"What makes us happy?" ... on our happiness: For information about the study and a link to Robert Waldinger's TED Talk, see Liz Mineo, "Good Genes Are Nice, but Joy Is Better," *Health & Medicine, The Harvard Gazette*, April 11, 2017, https://news.harvard.edu/gazette/story/2017/04/over-nearly-80-years-harvard-study-has-been-showing-how-to-live-a-healthy-and-happy-life/.

73 LISTEN TO WHAT YOU LISTEN TO
research on the effects of music: See, for example, "Mind, Body & Jazz: How Jazz Can Improve Your Health," Top Master's in Healthcare Administration, accessed May 21, 2019, https://www.topmastersin healthcare.com/mind-body-jazz/.
A study ... rock music: See Dorothy Retallack, *The Sound of Music and Plants* (Marina Del Rey, CA: DeVORSS & Co., 1973).

74 BE IN NATURE
Researchers have found: Danielle F. Shanahan et al., "Health Benefits from Nature Experiences Depend on Dose," *Scientific Reports* 6, (June 23, 2016), article 28551, https://doi.org/10.1038/srep28551.

78 SPEND TIME NEAR WATER
Some studies have shown: See Wallace J. Nichols, *Blue Mind: The Surprising Science That Shows How Being Near, In, On or Under Water Can Make You Happier, Healthier, More Connected, and Better at What You Do* (New York: Little, Brown and Company, 2014).

84 SURROUND YOURSELF WITH COLOR

even in lab studies: Keith W. Jacobs and James F. Suess, "Effects of Four Psychological Primary Colors on Anxiety State," *Perceptual and Motor Skills* 41, no. 1 (August 1, 1975): 207–10, https://doi.org/10.2466/pms.1975.41.1.207.

94 GET MORE SUN

Sunlight burns anxiety... into that sun: Randy A. Sansone and Lori A. Sansone, "Sunshine, Serotonin, and Skin: A Partial Explanation for Seasonal Patterns in Psychopathology?" *Innovations in Clinical Neuroscience* 10, nos. 7 and 8 (July/August 2013): 20–4.

98 HELP OTHERS

Some studies: See, for example, Christopher Bergland, "3 Specific Ways That Helping Others Benefits Your Brain," *Psychology Today*, February 21, 2016, https://www.psychologytoday.com/ca/blog/the-athletes-way/201602/3-specific-ways-helping-others-benefits-your-brain; and Tristin K. Inagaki et al., "The Neurobiology of Giving versus Receiving Support: The Role of Stress-Related and Social Reward–Related Neural Activity," *Psychosomatic Medicine* 78, no. 4 (May 2016): 443–53, https://doi.org/10.1097/PSY.0000000000000302.

Acknowledgments

WRITING THIS book has been a journey. There's the journey of the last two years which were *fully dedicated* to this book, the three years before that where I wrote another book that I never released (but part of which thematically lead to *Own Your Anxiety*), and the many years before that where I learned how to build a business, find a higher way of living, and connect to my true self while journeying through the stepping-stones of life.

I'm so deeply grateful for all of the support so many of you have shown me both in this writing process and also in helping me with Notable; forgive me if some names are left out. If you've never written one of these before, as a first-timer, let me tell you—it ain't easy!

I have to start by thanking my supportive and awesome brother, Thomas. You're always there for me, often in a moment's notice, bro. Us becoming closer and putting our differences behind us has been a true blessing *and* a lesson about how to live life. A massive thanks for always willing to read over my words whether it was for this book, my Life Letter, or anything else. You redefine what it means to be "selfless" and "loyal." I love you.

Mom, the last couple of years of your life have been your toughest yet. But you've chosen to also make them the most inspiring. You're a different person today than you were pre-cancer; the Universe is fortunate to have you as a valued member of it. You've continued to show GD that there is no challenge that you can't handle, and you've always shown me that love and communication is the way. You're getting better every day and I can't wait to see you in the front row on the book tour.

Dad, you have been someone I've always admired. You've been a role model since day one. Your tenacity for not letting the hand of life you were dealt dictate your future has inspired me literally my entire life. You didn't have to be the supportive, caring, selfless man who you are. Actually, *not* being the great person who you are would have been more expected based on your upbringing, but you created your own expectations of yourself and have always lived up to them. Your words of encouragement have always given me the extra energy I needed to push forward, even against the odds. I cherish every road trip and adventure that we've been on together. Thanks for always reminding me that I was given broad shoulders to carry the weight that sometimes we just need to carry.

Jennifer, not many people can call their stepmother a combination of being a family member and a dear friend. Your voice of reason, generosity, and hospitality has never gone unappreciated nor has your willingness to let me crash at the house whenever I've needed to!

Lisa and Ashley, I'm truly blessed to be able to call you my sisters. I cherish our relationship and am so proud of you both.

Joel Greenspan, I've never (I'm serious) met such a kind human in my life. You have been so good to my mother and

I will *always* be eternally grateful for you. There better be a quadruple king-size bed full of party sandwiches and Mashu Mashu waiting for you in Heaven.

Coby, Roo, Double, Meddy, you've been my brothers for twenty-plus years. Our bonds have often been my anchor even when I'm abroad. I'm so proud of who you've all become.

LTC4L.

Perz, you have been a best friend and confidant since 2009. We have had countless incredible times and so many vulnerable and authentic conversations. You're a true friend.

Oxman, I know we don't see each other much anymore and we live in opposite corners of the continent but my love for you is vast. You're one of the best humans I've ever had the privilege of meeting.

Ev, JM, Heath, Slots, Speis, and the rest of our NYC boys, I'm so lucky to have you in my life all of these years. Thanks for always taking me in with open arms, a place to crash, inspiring conversations, and great classes to sweat in.

Page Two Strategies fam!

Jesse, you've created a business that empowers us dreamers to share our dreams with the world. Thanks for being a caring, grounding, and wise partner to work with.

Rony, thanks for managing all of the moving parts so well—something that certainly isn't my strong suit. So happy for you as you take on the incredible opportunity to bring life into this world.

Kendra, I really loved our first meeting at Soho. Knowing that you would be editing this book and helping me articulate the important message contained in these pages has been a welcomed blessing.

Annemarie, you're so fun to work with! A true marketer—full of ideas and strategies. Thank you for cheering on my

outlandish marketing ideas too, and for all of your thoughtful work.

Peter, your designs are amazing. Thanks for the invaluable
design guidance and willingness to work with me on both the
little details and the big picture.

Taylor David, my bro. Thanks for the humor, amazing
energy, and the perfectly articulate logo that encapsulates my
message which you wouldn't let me pay you for. What a guy.

David Chilton, thanks for being willing to take my call! Your
guidance and support for this mission that I'm on has proved to
be so key in this process of learning how the book world works.
I'm indebted to you for your help. And Scott, I'm grateful that
we recently had the opportunity to become colleagues—lots
more to come. Guys, your online course is gold.

Amanda Lang, your belief in me expedited what I'm now
fortunate enough to be able to share with the world in a *huge*
way. Thanks for it all.

Nita Pronovost, thanks for your editorial and publishing
advice. You are amazing.

Zark, I love our friendship and am so grateful to watch you
continue to grow. Your growth is our growth.

Rabbi Jacobs, not only have you always been a loving force
for good and spiritual growth in my life, you've also been so
dedicated to your truth—a path of service. Within this truth I
have seen, again and again, my path.

Aryan, my yoga guru and brother! Who would have thought
that on a hungover Friday morning in Tel Aviv, I would find
you and that my life would forever change? I believe that GD
brought me to you and you to Israel for a reason. Your teach-
ings cemented my dedication to living a life of mind-body-soul
connection through the practice of yoga and more. I've never
let them go; in fact, I work on them daily. I'll see you in India
soon, brother. I truly love you.

Ron Reid and Marla Meenakshi Joy, you've been a constant reminder that you can do what you love and still build an amazing life. You've also shown me what a beautiful marriage can look like. Namaste!

Rabbi Oziel, your kindness and love is something I always feel. I have seen the path of service by watching you.

Dave Drutz, you've also never stopped being there to give me mentorship and support; I'm so grateful for that.

Dr. Harold Drutz, for always being there for us. For delivering me. For being a guardian to my mom.

Elena Brower—Wow, who are you?! How you did so much to help me out with this book process from the beauty and selflessness in your heart is a gesture that I shall never, ever forget. After Wanderlust a few years ago, you told me you'd make that intro when I was ready. You came through. And more. Every one of our calls and emails over the years during my authoring journey have always fueled me and filled me up. I'm eternally grateful.

Joe Mimran, for many, many years I have looked up to you. I admire the fact that you define what it means to be truly successful—yes, "making it in business" and *also* giving back to those around you. Now I have your name on the cover of my book and your valuable words inside of it. I suppose the very fact that this happened is both manifestation at work and testament that we can never stop believing in our dreams or ourselves.

Elaine Kunda, thank you for seeing something in me back when you became my "mentor" in 2009. You have no clue how much I benefited from having a kind, wise, and grounded mentor who believed in me, encouraged me, and guided me. We need more Elaines in this world.

Wanderlust Festival team, thank you for believing in me. Thank you for allowing me to join your family as a speaker when I was just getting started.

Music is such a key part of my life, I feel the desire to honor some of my "musical therapists":

Xavier Rudd, thank you for your brilliant artistry. Your music is my music. I'll never forget driving over two hours for your show and getting a spot in the front. Couldn't have been more grateful.

Jai-jagdeesh, for the angels you have birthed into the world. On those anxious mornings when what I needed most was to reconnect with my soul and to myself, your music has always given me permission and access back home.

Nahko and Medicine for the People, your music literally elevates me. Sometimes I feel like it was written for me or by me, that's how much I identify with most of your words. I'll be cheering you on as you build a movement. Maybe I'll be there with you.

Trevor Hall, Krishna Das, Rising Appalachia, Rebelution, Soja, thank you for keeping me connected.

Genny Miller, you showed up for me when I needed to show up for Mom. Thank you.

Blake Larson, Justin Roberts, Sabina Sohail, you were all with me at the beginning of this journey. For a while each one of you was literally the only person I worked with, and you may not fully know this, but your presence was so deeply appreciated.

Dale Carnegie for putting me on the journey at a young age to learn that everything begins with the power of a thought.

Bryce Courtenay for writing *The Power of One*. It took me two years to read, and that was on my *second* attempt, at sixteen years old; the inspiration gleaned from your book will last a lifetime.

Robin Sharma, *The Monk Who Sold His Ferrari* is a work that I leaned on to get me through the hard times I found myself in when trying to find grounding while going after the "entrepreneurial dream." I took it across Canada while I traveled cross-country to build up Notable. Today I still go to it just to keep me on the path. I've always seen a little Julian Mantle in me. Thanks for trusting in your path so that we can walk with you on it.

Michael A. Singer, I appreciate you putting *The Untethered Soul* and *The Surrender Experiment* into the world more than words can describe. Thank you for enabling me to truly grow.

Tony Robbins! Over eleven years ago I started to follow your work, attend your seminars, and implement many of your life strategies. They have done so much for me.

Gabby Bernstein, you have been a role model and mentor in this industry from afar. I've often found that your story is my story. I've held your books closely during various challenging times and am grateful for what you do. I look forward to collaborating.

DLE, thanks for believing.

To the old team at Notable. Wow, how many memories and experiences did we live through together? Thank you for standing by me for so many years. Your dedication and positivity helped me get through some of the challenging times and chapters that I share in this book.

I'd like to acknowledge and directly thank my senior staff for sticking with me for so many years (in order of tenure): Christian Nathler, Erin Davis, Karolina Jez, Philippe Maurer, and Eric Wainwright.

To Carli and Claire for acquiring Notable and making it better than ever.

To my former clients at Notable, I cannot thank you enough for believing. You had countless other places to invest your precious dollars but you chose to believe in my team and me.

About the Author

AS THE FOUNDER and former CEO of an award-winning
Canadian media company, Julian Brass understands the
importance of owning anxiety, both professionally and
personally. Julian moved back to Canada more than ten years
ago, after working in Silicon Valley and Florida for several
years, to be a part of, and contribute to, what was then just a
budding internet tech scene. He saw that there wasn't a single
online brand dedicated to inspiring driven Millennials to live a
notable life, so he created the Notable Awards and Notable.ca,
which today is Notable Life.

Shortly after launching Notable in 2008, Julian experienced severe anxiety for the first time and became determined
to deal with it naturally. This led him on an ever-expanding
journey, on which he simultaneously managed and grew his
former business while exploring empowering natural lifestyle
changes, such as holistic health and wellness, self-care, spirituality, yoga, and positive psychology.

This path to higher consciousness became Julian's way of
living.

Over the years, Julian has gone on to train and collaborate
with yogis from India, rabbis and priests in Jerusalem, top

medical doctors in New York City, and some of the most successful entrepreneurs in the world. Upon awakening to his mission to help people learn to help themselves own anxiety, he sold Notable in 2017 to dedicate his life to the path of service.

Today, he helps people all over the world #OwnYourAnxiety by guiding them toward empowering, natural tools, combining medical research from the West and holistic philosophies from the East. These tools, which are the foundation of the Own Your Anxiety method, lead to a redefined relationship with anxiety, taking it from negative and debilitative to positive and facilitative. As an international keynote speaker, workshop facilitator, coach, teacher, and healer, Julian aims to leave every person he connects with ready not just to own anxiety, but to own themselves holistically, just a bit more so that they can truly *own their lives.* You can follow Julian on Instagram and Twitter at @JulianBrass.

OwnYourAnxiety.com
JulianBrass.com